# Magic Carpet

## Selected Poems

## River Mary Malcolm

iUniverse, Inc.
New York   Bloomington

**Magic Carpet**
**Selected Poems**

*iUniverse books may be ordered through booksellers or by contacting:*

*iUniverse*
*1663 Liberty Drive*
*Bloomington, IN 47403*
*www.iuniverse.com*
*1-800-Authors (1-800-288-4677)*

*Because of the dynamic nature of the Internet, any Web addresses or links contained in this book may have changed since publication and may no longer be valid.*

*ISBN: 978-1-4401-2580-5 (pbk)*
*ISBN: 978-1-4401-2581-2 (ebk)*

*Printed in the United States of America*

*iUniverse rev. date: 2/24/2009*

# Contents

# Dedication

This book is for my father, David Donald Malcolm, 1916-2008, the first to teach me to love poetry.

Letting Go
        *for my father*
        (2009)

My memory started to fumble early in my mid-life.
Whole parts of my history vanished like stars on a cloudy night.

Today, I go into our staffroom to find
the things that I brought from my father's kitchen

are gone. I can't even remember the specifics of what's missing –
forks, spoons, knives, mugs, glasses, plates, serving dishes –

small humble objects that his hands
lifted and held, week after week, year after year,

objects that I carefully packed, when we emptied
his condominium, into a box to bring back to the staffroom.

He didn't care for fancy new things, but he loved
these simple objects in his own kitchen.

When I touched them, I touched his love.
They remembered his fingers.

Where did they go–these things, these living
reminders, remainders, of him?  Who,

among my coworkers, took them or threw them away?
I imagine his hand reaching up through swirling waters

and my hand unable to reach–where did they go,
these living reminders, remainders, of him?

They are gone. Forget my rage, my urge to
investigate, explain, punish, fix, blame.

They are gone. Even though I can't even remember
their names, my hand in this poem can reach

through the clouds and into the darkness
of night, to release these invisible stars.

# Acknowledgements

I am indebted to many who have supported my writing over the years, including Judy Malcolm, Chris Downing, Jim Kissane, Lynda Koolish, Holaday Mason, JoEllen Moldoff, Caroline Buchanan, and many more whose loving kindness has nourished and sustained me. I especially thank my father, David Malcolm; my mother, Virginia Flanagan; and my teacher-poet-friend, Linda Brown, who are no longer living. I miss them.

To those who lovingly labor to keep small publications afloat so that poems can have an embodied existence in this world, I bow in gratitude and thank them for the previously published poems that are reprinted here. With apologies to those I may have forgotten, I offer special thanks to *San Diego City Schools Creative Writing magazine, Grinnell College Review, Golden Hills Poetry Express, Feminist Communications, Golden Kimono, Magee Park Poets, Art Music and Poetry Unlimited, South Coast Poetry, Calyx, New York Quarterly,* and *Poetry Motel*, Also to the anthology, *Claiming the Spirit Within: A Sourcebook of Women's Poetry*, and to Chris Downing for inclusion in her books, *Myths and Mysteries of Same Sex Love, The Long Journey Home, Gods in Our Midst*.

My deepest gratitude is to language itself and to all the ancestors who have passed the miracle of speech down to me, and to all the poets who passed along the wisdom and wild ways to use language itself to transform the wounds that life (and language itself) inevitably inflicts on the human spirit. I cannot repay my debt to the poets I have loved. I bow in gratitude, happy to receive their generosity, happy to give back what I can.

I gratefully acknowledge the generosity of photographer Ken Crawford, www.rdelsol.com, for allowing me to use his astrophotograph for the back cover.

# The Twisting Path

**The Twisting Path**
*for John teaching yoga in Cambridge, 1970*
(1993)

In a church basement in Harvard Square,
architect by day, yogi by night, John
teaches yoga for free, two nights
a week, staring so unblinkingly
into our eyes that I picture an
owl unflinching and flooded by light.

"Yoga says practicing asanas isn't
competitive, not like Western athletics."
John speaks as if he's no more than a
conduit for tradition, though his erect
spine, legs crossed into double lotus, give his
conduit the pizzazz of a pretzel. "Yoga says
it's not about perfecting the outer form,
it's about being aware of your own
experience. You are the path."

From my newcomer's mat, I gaze at
each exactly posed body, precise yet
unpredictable, origami taking shape
from a flat paper square, how it folds
and unfolds, stretches, twists, curves,
into cobra, scorpion, lion, fish, tree,
becomes elemental, not human, changeable
as the wind or the sea. I glimpse
what a twisting path I am likely to be.

**The Knife**
   (1993)

Her five-year-old fingers curl
around the wood handle of a knife,
just the right size for her hand. Carefully
nudging the pointed tip, the narrow gleam
of the blade, the keen edge of danger
that makes her mother say "no," making
it far fairer than knives she's permitted to hold.

With this knife, she need never fear being
called a baby again. If her big sister teased,
she could silence her with a stroke. The way
that big sister cut off her hair with scissors one day,
with this knife she could cut open her big sister's throat.
With this knife, she could protect her own
baby sister from every monster on earth.

She could tell the Big People what to do,
with this knife. If they didn't, she could
cut off their toes. It would be the law
of the small, the Big People would be
overthrown and have to do whatever
the Small People told them to. They couldn't
touch knives, and they would have to eat
everything on their plates, and go to bed
when the Small People said, and
when they wanted a drink of water
the Small People would say "Just go to sleep."

Right now she's going to carve this pumpkin
all by herself. She'll just stick the knife
in right here to cut out an eye and she'll cut. . .
and she'll carve. . . but it's stuck, she can't
get it out, and her mother is coming
her mother has hung up the phone
so she'll grab the knife tight
and she'll pull and she'll twist and she'll pull
until it comes out.
There it is!

4

All clear,
except for this baby finger of hers,
gushing blood
she starts to scream "Mommy!
I want my Mommy!"
her big sister rolling her eyes
as she sneers "What
a baby you are."

### Christina's World

*for the young crippled woman in Wyeth's painting*
(1980)

Your sister counts the things you cannot do.
She gathers wood, washes, cooks, cans, cleans,
and every morning helps dress you.
The tally, grown too large, swarms
from her eyes.

Breathing hard,
arms unsteady,
you creep
half-snake without scales or grace,
you drag your thighs, your legs, your feet
across fields bristling with wheat.
Small rocks scrape through
the fabric of your dress.

The house diminishes.
Wind unravels your hair,
your breath.
Your eyes caress
the horizon.

## The Jack O'Lantern
### (1974)

1.
 A grown-up knife in a little girl's hand
carving out features for a pumpkin-man
slipped.
Cut into the hand.

A surgical needle in a specialist's hand
connecting severed tendons in a hurt little hand,
steady.
Rescued the hand.

2.
Twenty-one years of scar tissue later
I met you.
I asked you to be my new surgeon
and heal my soul.

You aren't what I expected.
You keep handing me tools.
Surgery I trust—
surgery by a specialist,
but not by me.

Listen: the tools of transformation
are dangerous.
They cut the hand that uses them.

You say I must risk it.
You see how afraid I am.

3.
It is harvest time.
We sit together in a pumpkin patch.
You sit on a pumpkin-seat, laughing.
I say they aren't ripe.
You say they will die on the vine.
You say things are constantly changing.

I say what a shame for such pumpkins
to be open and empty,
carved with a garish face,
a candle placed
in the center where seeds ought to be.

You say they will die on the vine.
You say things are constantly changing.

4,
You put a knife in my hand
and leave me alone.
What else can I do? I start carving.

The face is finished.
It is not what I thought.
The light inside gives it a glow.
The features are someone I know.
It's not a bad lot for a pumpkin.

I look at my hands:
not a child's anymore.
Not a surgeon's, either,
but they'll do.

## After Mary Died
### (1993)

The day Mary died, I was in Boston
planning a new life. When I came back
she was dead, and all Madison collapsed
to the little apartment
she died in, upstairs porch-room
with its long row of windows,
white curtains billowing.

Later on, I'd put a belt around my neck,
pulling it tight, just to contemplate Mary's courage,
how she died not by hanging, not by leaping
into the arms of gravity, but by leaning slowly
away from the fastened end of a rope;
her own hand steadily, deliberately, and to
the last breath, tightened the noose.

I'd study the logistics of hanging, search
the ceiling for something secure enough
to suspend myself from. Just my luck,
there was nothing.

## Two Marys in Madison, Wisconsin
   (2000)

Thirty years ago Mary
you were only a girl of 20
with my same name,
with your pale porcelain face
and your farm girl freckles.

We rode the bus
through the Madison summer night
to watch DH Lawrence's *Sons and Lovers*
made into a movie
and I remember, still, certain angles of camera:
pan of a graveyard, close-up of two men wrestling,
wrestling in a way that left me unsure to this day
just where the boundary lay
between making love and making war.

That was 1970, "Make Love Not War"
the mantra of our generation, and just about then
I'd begun to doubt if we really did
know the difference, if anyone did.

After the union picnic - when we'd won,
or thought that we'd won
the teaching assistants' strike -
Pointing at my dish
for the potluck, "Should
I leave it?" I said.
"If you leave it, it's litter,"
the union president,
who was cleaning up,
said. But I was off
on a mescaline trip,
rushing into the arms of death,
falling deeply in love with death.
I could see a place
full of freedom and light,
clear of history's burden,
the bombs and dying children

captured on camera.

I could see moments in time flash by
like cards being shuffled;
between them,
the shimmer of death - eternity -
the unbroken home
I'd always wanted.
"If you leave it, it's litter,"
the union president said
and I thought he meant
my life.

I yearned in those days for death.
I began to read Sylvia Plath,
and the dream of death seemed to me
refuge, a sweet place to hide
while the bombs kept on falling.
When the U.S. invaded Cambodia,
we student radicals rampaged the night,
and though I didn't pick up a single stone
and hurl it through a single window,
I became part of the seething churning charging beast
that furiously smashed as it moved,
and I did breathe the tear gas and weep
as part of that mob.

Soon the young men of the Students
for a Democratic Society dreamed
not of women, but of testing the muscle
of their young manhood against some physical foe.
I didn't know then the shame that they felt
for escaping Vietnam, the need
to prove something elemental and male
in the face of all they'd been spared.
Their way to "Make Love Not War"
became to dream of brawls and broken windows
and bombs of their own, and for me, death sang
between the razor thin moments of time
more and more sweetly.

Riding home on the bus after the movie,
we spoke of suicide, Mary, casually,
of how we would do it, if we were to try,
and I enjoyed the chance to rub my tongue,
to test my teeth
on the texture of words
that touched death, my new love,
to taste the tension between your freckles
and our taboo conversation,
and never once dreamed
you would actually do it.

White curtains billow
from the long row of open windows
in the upstairs room where you lived, as if
the summer breeze wants to go on breathing for you,
for the young girl
who fastened the rope to the door,
and to her own neck,
and then held,
and leaned down,
and went on leaning and holding
as she must have been
gasping for breath,
as, like the wrestlers in the movie,
the animal in her
must have been flailing and fighting
against the resolve.

I made a painting of you, Mary,
from a high school photo your sister found:
your smile wide as the sky,
your teeth holding a daffodil,
the black of eternity just behind.
And when it was over, all I could think
was how strong you had been,
how the wrong Mary survived.

After you died, a radical's bomb exploded
in Army Math Research Center
and killed a young father.

Not that my hand held the match
to the fuse, just that I know I belong
to the seething churning charging beast
that smashes as it goes.

A year or two later, I walked down
my own inner road to the river,
my pockets filled
with a heavy cargo of stone.
It was as if I became Virginia Woolf,
relived her dying as my own.
Three days later, on an acid trip,
I rose to new life,
my new name the water
in which my former self drowned.

Somehow, Mary,
I found the strength
to fasten a rope
to the door of the future,
to wrap that rope
around my own neck,
and then hold,
and lean forward,
lean forward
into the unknown,
lean forward
into responsibility
in a world I lack
the power to redeem,
to go on leaning
and holding
as, like the wrestlers
in the movie,
the innocent animal in me
flails and fights
to be free.

## After Mr. Goodbar
### (1980)

The town she came from vanished
after Mr. Goodbar killed her friend.
She went back to take photographs of home:
it left no images on film.
She thought of home as mythical, deep South:
a gracious place that never had existed.

She was a waif in Greenwich village; there, the rescuers
of derelicts and junkies tried, with marijuana, to save
her from an opposite oblivion. They gently peeled off
her pure white gloves. She smiled, as if to thank them,
but her teeth chattered terror. Later, she learned to
grit the teeth. As for her ungloved hands, they were fans
in a geisha girl dance she exchanged for conversation.

She studied the popular paths to peace–marijuana, meditation,
jogging–made lists of them she followed all day long,
checking off items, trying diligently to relax.

Born in 1943, she felt guilty for keeping silent about
the Jews, although at the time she was too young to speak.
She felt guilty for Mr. Goodbar, too.

**For Kathleen**
    *on the day of her first trick*
    (1974)

These dollars pry open your thighs
and come inside—
they live and grow
and feed on you like worms.
Now you *know*
what a prostitute is.

These dollars pry open my brain
and come inside.
They live and grow
and feed on me like worms.
Now I *know*
what a Ph.D. is.

These dollars devour your cunt.
These dollars devour my mind.

Oh my sister we are the same.
Sold and bought.

No diaphragm guards my brain.
No K-Y jelly lets him come in
                      frictionlessly.

I wonder
is it better to sell out your way?

No words guard your cunt.
No phony status allows you to sin
                      virtuously.

You know you're a whore. You say
any day God may
in His holy rage strike you down.

I think about god: a warm
heart where torn

15

opposites rest, arm in arm.
She will not strike you down.

Sister one day
when we make enough more
we will buy ourselves back
and be free.
And take over our world,
you and me.

**Private, Not for Sharing**
        (1976)

I try to understand these new times,
see them fresh.
They do resemble
other times I've known
the way, after you've seen so many,
new faces start to resemble the old.
I get to thinking people repeat themselves,
there are only so many kinds.
After you meet them all
they circle back like a merry-go-round.

Sometimes you girls remind me of us.
Growing up in the twenties,
we were pretty sure of ourselves,
we rode the crest of a new era,
our lives were not our mothers' lives.
We wanted to leave the city, just like you.

But no. It was different then.
I never wanted to be a
lesbian.
We abhorred the word,
our love for each other
was an unnatural inescapable doom.
We tried to escape it.
I slept with Lily's husband that one time
just to feel the faint trace of her touch
on his skin.
We never even whispered
that word
you girls walk so proudly in.

Forty years.

Do you remember, Lily, the farm in Georgia,
me with my fancy roses,
you breeding afghan dogs,
the days   the months   the years

you spent bent over the typewriter
after the roses failed and the dogs
and we agreed you were the finer writer
so it was me sent back to work
to keep you writing.

But what an adventure it was in the early days.
Your sleek dogs, and my soft roses.
You loved to come and kiss me in the greenhouse
while I watered the young ones.
"Do you love your roses better?"
You once said.
You were so soft and round,
your eyes always laughing.
I was lean and serious,
the way your leaping dogs looked
when they began to get sick from the poison
the neighbors left out for them.

We were two against the world.
We survived that way twenty-five years,
the longest marriage in my family,
survived the family whispers
repeated to us by the children
not understanding the words they repeated,
survived, gritted our teeth, survived.
For twenty-five years Father introduced you
as my "business partner."

You kept on writing.
Through the thirties
through the forties
no one but me to
read your writings to,
I encouraged you, but
ten years passed and twenty.

The fifties.
Can you imagine
your writing
lithe and elegant as your afghan hounds,

sensual as my roses,
streaking through that dull silence?
You'd have gashed open their sky
loud as the Fourth of July
they could never have patched it closed
with their star-spangled banners.

But no. It didn't happen.
Your dogs were gone and my flowers,
then finger by finger you began to disappear.
Your nights stiffened,
demons with yellow eyes
pulled on your sleeves,
sometimes my face melted into theirs.
I held your body taut and trembling with terror
like a plucked guitar string
through all the long nights.

I wanted to help you, Lily.
You and I
were the one true color in a faded place.

I wanted to stay with you, Lily,
didn't you know?
But I had to go.

It was we two against the world.
But the world broke through
the fragile shell we had enclosed it in,
it dripped its horrors into your life.
After all those years of writing your heart out, Lily,
and not getting read,
it wasn't your mind that was ill,
it was the world.

I wasn't strong enough
I couldn't hold back the world
I couldn't take care of you.
After twenty-five years
I abandoned you.

These young girls now,
so many of them.
They have each other.
Fields and fields of roses,
a sea of playful afghan hounds.
They are wild and free,
they are proud of themselves and each other.
They are brown from the sun,
from walking outside arm in arm.

I'm an old woman now, and old women
can't help rubbing their fingertips
lovingly against those two little words
"what if"
hour after hour, like rubbing
an old prayer stone.

But Lily, what if we had lived now,
how would our lives have been?

## Eleanor's Poem
### (1980)

Hicks, love, our secret's out.
Everyone knows it
except those who are stopping
their ears with fear.
The young girls march in the street
they carry our faces like banners
we have given them images
footsteps to walk in
models of powerful women
shaping forces in politics and journalism
drawing sustenance from
each other. Darling
they celebrate us
like a circus, a ritual,
reenact our passion among
themselves
touch breasts exactly as we did
lips to soft skin
gentle fingers between tender lips
into our secret place.
We are curled now in that pink cave
that we learned our way to when alive,
eternity.
The young girls visit us here
and draw the threads of our lives,
our love, onward
into the future.

Hicks, dear, it's Eleanor.
You know all this commotion
about whether our love
was consummated
in the flesh
whether we shared the touch
of fingers lips breast,
whether we shared
and no one, the fools,
even raises eyebrows

at our thousands of letters.
The words, Hicks, the words
with you to make my solitude full
reflecting my day
naming my experience
I claimed the language
and there they are still
fretting and afraid we claimed
our bodies –
we did that *young*, dear, didn't we,
then spent the remaining years
claiming ourselves. Together,
claiming our lives,
the words, the letters,
the passion of naming,
the ardor of love at a distance.
You making my solitude full
knowing my value
someone wanting me
wanting me to be all that I could
wanting me to put words on my day
name my experience.
There was a reason, Hicks,
no other president's wife
was a force of her own.
They didn't have you, darling,
thirsty for their thoughts,
for their words.
Your love to grow into,
all the room and distance
you gave, always surrounded by love.
They didn't have your passionate tongue
the intelligent hollows of your ears
they didn't have
two women's minds wed,
twined in a long slow passion,
they didn't have what we have, Hicks,
even now the love of a lifetime,
love of the ripening years,
love that loves distances
the daily letters, exchanges,

the shared solitudes,
and the rare occasional sweet body embraces.

They've opened our letters, Hicks,
the fragrance of tranquility
seeps out of them
into this strange new dimension
we occupy. I've gotten
used to being without a body, dear,
no arms, thighs, tongue, fingers
to communicate with,
but I haven't been able to
let go of words. Words, Hicks,
words were our secret. Words
were the pink secret cave
in which we lost ourselves
to ecstasy. It was each
other's solitudes we touched,
entered, emerged from, ah, deeper
than vaginas will ever be, for
all the pulsations of flesh,
the wonderful crevices of the brain,
those secret caves into which we crept
entered and knew each other
with words, darling,
learned to take power with words,
learned how to know, how to name,
became real to ourselves,
were suddenly living our actual lives
as so few women in history
ever have done.
Ah Hicks, dear, you entered me
I entered you
we became one again and again.
A lion because of your love
I found the voice of my secret self,
my roar,
I took my place in the state.

They have opened our letters.
The world is learning our secret.

Everyone knows, except those
who have stopped up their ears.
It wasn't when you loved me
with thighs and tongue and lips
and fingers, when you explored
my body and helped me learn
the geography of my pleasure,
though you did that so tenderly well, dear,
don't ever think I can forget that symphony,
your caresses,
but it wasn't that, Hicks,
that wasn't the secret.
The secret was words:
shared solitudes.
We bequeath these letters now to the
new generations, strong young women who come after
growing to fill wider solitudes
than we ever imagined.
They have won their lives for themselves
they've learned the art of sharing
across the enormous distances
they need for their growing.
We bequeath them our letters,
path breakers, lovers, women of letters.

Ah Hicks doesn't it bring back
some of the fire
feeling them open our letters
take our words into their lives
inherit our strength?
The words have a life of their own.

## Cross-Country Motorcycle Trip
*for Patricia*
(1993)

Across miles and days, my arms encircle
your waist, while my thighs hum
with each vibration and surge
of the engine you drive
and I, your passenger, survey
the slender symmetry of your ribs.
Even O'Keefe could not paint
their complete simplicity, their
quiet curve.

You drive like a lullaby, leaning
and leading me into the arc
of your turn,
brakes soft as a mother
kissing goodnight.

Winding among redwoods,
shooting through Oregon desert,
unrolling our sleeping bags
randomly at roadsides
covered by darkness and stars
with only the rustling of wild things
as they move all night through the grass
disturbing our sleep.
Your trusting body
which never was raped
melts into earth, while mine
braces to meet
all I cannot lock out.

Only in Yellowstone I relax,
where park rangers, campgrounds,
vacationing families, the pure
profusion of nature promises safety.
I wake from deep sleep to find you
sitting upright, flashlight in hand,
searching in terror for bears.

You are not a stunt driver. We don't
drive the bike over cliffs of many colors
to tumble down with falling water, don't
stampede the once great buffalo herds,
don't join the moose wading the river
through early morning mist, but the beauty
of the place creates sacredness I can't help
but grow one with: I become bubbling
mud pots, hot turquoise springs, shooting
geysers. I tremble under your touch.

And then the endless hour by hour trek over the flat
unchanging plain – Montana, South Dakota, Minnesota –
where your hero arms, hard-muscled as any man's, refuse
to tire, but your patience frays when I beg
for rest, my untoughened body throbbing
with aches and pains. "You want the whole
world to be Yellowstone," you accuse,
and you're right.

I remember the time your touch first
took me to places I'd never been,
and I wept. Unnerved by my tears
"I'll give you something to cry about,"
you said. And you did.

## Love Letter to The Lesbian Community
   (2002)

I met you first in Cambridge, 1974:
playful party of feminist dykes
flirting and arguing about "butch"
and "fem." I was roommate, friend,
never before had I seen women
treat women as sexual, exciting,
desirable, worthy to come first
in each other's lives. Yearning vaguely
for you all my life, I had felt so
alone. You were my welcome
home, my first mirror, permission
to be who I am, first glimpse that
my most shameful and impossible needs
might transform into proud satisfaction.

Lesbian community, my first sweet taste
of you infected me with hope and self-love,
I danced singing down the halls
of Massachusetts Institute of Technology.
I stood on my head, I broke up
with my boyfriend,
told everyone I met I was lesbian -
though I'd not tasted breast or vagina
of any individual woman.

You–"the community"–you
huddled to decide who'd take
the risk, who'd "bring me out."
It was almost as if the first time
I touched the slippery smooth
warmth inside a vagina, so
pillowy and stretchy, such give -
almost as if it belonged not only
to that first woman, but to you,
to the whole community - the warm softness of
breasts, my fingers and tongue newly exploring
this most ancient territory, so
powerful and mysterious, such

a reflection of my own body, no longer
an object to be ranked and compared,
an object of barter and shame, ogling
and fear, that men made it seem,
but my female body, opening to an ocean,
deep cave of life, cauldron of
magic, place of power,
palace of pleasure, temple
of transformation.

I met you again, lesbian community, in
the first women's bar I ever went inside,
*The Saints* in Boston, where I tried
to break up a fight and ended up
with a circle of teeth mark bruises
on my thigh for my effort. I was
young, I had never seen
women fight.

More than my body, you,
lesbian community, you
were the first to mirror my words.
First to listen to my words and not judge,
not make them into objects
to be ranked and compared,
first to see them like vaginas–
as the edge of the ocean,
the cave of life–to hear the original
joy and power I felt in them,
to listen not with intellect alone
but with belly and heart, and then
to embody and live them.

## Other Lives
### (2002)

In late October I decide to wade
into the wind of old
and harsh decisions unfinished although made.

Walking on fallen gold
I crush and grind no matter what I will
more than I hold.

If other selves find lives I waste or spill
oh may they find them sweet
and live them: laugh and eat and drink their fill

and walking down some long familiar street
with every step I take
may I be wide awake in case we meet

for though our hearts might break
if we glimpsed clearly lives we cannot trade
we'd love ours–for the other's sake.

## With Michelle at Hiram Brown's Grave
   (1980)

"He lived his convictions.
Pioneer abolitionists
persecuted for remembering
those in bonds
as bound with them.
His motto:
One world at a time."

Grass grows over earth
that long ago swallowed him.
A century later, we pass.

I watch that great bear, Michelle's body,
guard her bashful child heart.
In her art, Michelle cuts up maps,
pastes places together,
creates jazz collage.
She paints bright melodies,
rivers to run through
the sectioned harmony of city blocks.
She composes from multiplicity:
more than one world.

The music she paints
grants her courage. She lives,
in a time much more chaotic than his,
as simply as Hiram Brown lived.

## String Quartet in E Minor

*for Bedrich Smetana, who died completely deaf and suffering
from hallucinations in an asylum (for the "insane") in Prague,
60 years old, May 12, 1884.*
(1993)

Eight years before you die,
deaf, music career at an end,
three of your daughters dead,
your faithful wife dead,
you compose your life's music.

*Allegro vivo appassionato*
Sweet yearning of youth, arms outstretched
to music, to art, as if to bodies of lilacs
whose fragrance you clasp to your chest.

*Allegro moderato a la Polka*
Music as waves on which your own body
lifts and is tossed, as you dance dance dance
the night that goes on forever
in the arms of the girl you love.

*Largo sostenuto*
Spilling over from fullness, the cello's dark throb,
the sigh of the violin, the long slow lullaby of a marriage
that soothes even now the terrible trembling of your heart.

*Finale vivace*
Folk music: the people
breathing their lives into your music,
passing their spirit on
                into
              sudden
              silence
          Shriek in high E, then
          The sound of young lilacs
          The dance of first love
        The long lullaby of marriage
      Folk music, breath of the people
          broken, vanished

## To Dementia
### (1966)

Demons come and demons go—
world, don't regret it.
Demons laugh and leer and crow
insolent, because they know
they can wander someone's seeming
lost from strayest paths and gleaming
lost and wild and woolly mad
drowned in brooks, afield, and glad.
Oh Dementia! Come and fetch me
now, before the world can catch me.
Real Madness, I implore
open your enchanting door.
Let me scream and stamp and holler,
bite my toes and tear my collar.
I have tantrums ripe with age
and I'd love it in a cage.

Show me sunsets demons see
Fill me with demonic glee
and the crazy laughter
jumbled up with grief
knowing death comes after
(does it hurt?)   but listen:
Life can sear and it can glisten
strained to the lute of lunacy
it can give a whole new music
sounds that only demons hear.

Things that only demons know
sane men never wonder
artists, yes, can still be healthy
one or two were even wealthy
but there are sunsets only madmen see,
and the mad alone can know
how the world flies to pieces
watching as they watch a show
living lives like leases.

It may be that some are happy
always staid and true.
If I loved the sunshine only
then I might be too.
But I love the palaces,
mossy, shadowed, strange.
That's why I cry madness,
long to be deranged.

When I've seen the sights and visions
known the splendor and the pain
then perhaps and if I like it
I'll try being sane.

## What It's All About
(1977)

Lou says, "I used to work in this building years ago,
when it took up the whole block.
Smith and Frye, it was linotype then.
They went out of business after 70 years,
couldn't compete with the new offset presses.

"Sure, I'm in the union.
I'm a journeyman, set type my whole life.
What I liked best was being the lock-in man,
you know what I mean, not doors,
we had these big metal frames of type,
            this big,
thirty-two magazine pages.
I had to lift up the edges, like this,
make sure all the type was locked in.
Do you know how to tell if you've got the right pages?
The even-numbered ones go on the right,
and the numbers add up to one more
than the length of the book.
Bet you didn't know that.
Say you had thirty-two pages, then
one and thirty-two would go side by side,
add up to thirty-three, you see
what I mean?

"I've been in the union since 1945.
Sure, I was already skilled,
took classes all through junior high, high school,
then nine years in the navy.
I'm in the union still, I get the magazine.
I see all the new machines they're using,
but, look here, seeing pictures isn't the same as doing.
Besides that, I'm an old man,
I don't want to learn all those things.
I'm 62, do you think they'd hire me?
No, they want to train a young man
with a future, so they'll make money off him,
that's what it's all about.

"So I'm a cook now. Look, I'm learning all kinds
of new things, doing a job I've never done before.
You know, for me it's exciting.
I never chose to be a printer anyhow,
there were all the shops in school–
wood, electric, printing, shoemaking–
you know, I thought
I wanted to go into shoes.
I used to nail new heels on my shoes
during the depression.
I was always proud of that.
But I did well in print shop,
so I stayed with it.

"What I really wanted to do
was play baseball.
But I was 28 after the war
too old for ball.
I went to L.A. anyway, to be an umpire
one summer, and quit Smith and Frye.
After that, they wouldn't take me back.

"So I went up to the union office in L.A.,
there was this ad for a job in Santa Ana,
so I called.
'How soon can you get here?' he said.
I'd had a few beers, so I stalled.
I don't drink anymore, but I used to drink then.
So I told him tomorrow.
'How soon can you start work?' he asked
when I got there,
and I stalled him again,
I didn't start until the day after.
That night I ate in the small café
and asked the pretty waitress for a date.
We saw each other every day after that
for three months, and then we got married.
I'd been with girls from all over the world,
but this was different.
I was in love.

We were married 17 years,
'til she died of cancer.

"Listen, I'm going to go now.
Young person like you,
you've got better things to do
than listen to an old man talk.
But let me tell you one thing,
you're really going to succeed in this world.
I mean that, not many young people
would listen to an old man talk.
You're going to succeed in this world."

## On the Island of Dreams
### (1990)

I first saw the island, Peter,
through you.
After you found your cabin
you carried the island's beauty everywhere
a pure light that shone through your eyes
and reached everyone near you.
You carried your island future, expectant,
a slight secret smile brushed your lips
like the face of a woman with child
a faraway look,
as if listening to the sea,
to the future,
to the tiny stranger inside her.

When in time I lifted my own eyes to these towering trees
these deep fir and cedar,
when I traced this pale lichen on their trunks
touched the profusion of these ground ferns
heard the continual trickle of water seeking the sea
rested my eyes on this quiet pond,
when I stood in this wood
in the heart of a fairy tale from Grimm
or beyond Grimm,
this wood deeper and taller,
touching the sky,
so far beyond the scale of the human,
I scarcely stood as high as a fir tree's thumb.

By then you'd traded your pregnant woman's smile
for the worn exhaustion of a toddler's parent -
your child's hands in everything,
its constant opposition.
The dream became real.
Dreams are like that, they grow
as children do.
They are constantly wrestling us
to recognize their changed being.

And we tag after them
dying again and again
to our old selves
grasping at the original form of the dream
and we manage somehow
to choose the life of the dream
it's growing motion
over the empty form
where we once thought it beckoned.

We choose life somehow,
which is constantly changing,
over death,
that sweet stillness,
for only when we breathe our last breath
and depart from our lives on that breath,
do we settle
almost motionless
as the island mist
settles
slowly
in the tops
of these island trees.

Until then
we tag after our dreams
standing scarcely as tall as their thumbs.

## My Great Uncle Spike
### *for Marcus Bond*
(2002)

At the family wedding
my great uncle Spike
in his black pants and suspenders
looked just like a fireman
only without the vest and the hat.
It was at Dave and Buster's
where they have a restaurant
with a pool table.
The family was all there
of course
it being a family wedding.
I usually don't go
to those family things,
I didn't go to the funeral
for Great Uncle Spike
after he was dead.
I thought it would be boring,
and sad. But I'm getting ahead.
At the family wedding
Uncle Spike was still alive.

We played a game of pool.
He won of course
because I really stink, I mean
I was really new. I'd played
maybe twenty times.
We own a pool table
but my brother Will
used to cover it up
with all of his crayons.
That kid could be an artist
if he knew how to color
inside the lines.

Great Uncle Spike
showed me how to hold
the cue in one hand

39

and let it slide
between the fingers
of my other hand.
That way I could
hit the ball right
in the solid center
and it made a great
solid sound and rolled
smoothly down the
green felt of the table in just
the direction I sent it.

Someday I'll play a great
game of pool and it will
be all because of my
great Uncle Spike.

His birthday was September
eleventh, and when they crashed
those two planes full of people
into those two high towers
full of people too, and had
people falling and dying
everywhere and all of grownups
even the firemen were afraid,
I just wanted to tell him
how sorry I was that it had to be
on his birthday.

My own birthday came
just five days later,
and it wasn't very happy.
Two of my friends
couldn't come because
people they knew had
just died.

I wanted to tell my great
Uncle Spike how sorry
I was that it had to be
on his birthday. But

the doctors messed up,
they didn't do the right tests,
they said he was fine,
and a month later he died.
I wanted to tell him
how sorry I was,
but I didn't have time.

## At the Dentist's
      (1993)

"I'd like to go into trance, so
I'll be gone for the duration.
Don't bother to ask if you're
hurting me. I'll let you know."
Closing my eyes, I begin
to disappear.

Meanwhile, the dentist: "I know
just what you mean, I have
this dentist friend who comes
from Northern California.
I'm especially careful with him,
a dentist himself, you understand.
When I ask if I'm hurting him,
he says 'don't bother me, I'm
running through the redwoods,
having a wonderful time.'"

My eyes close. I sink down
to my roots, down to
where I can float on soothing
waters of my own secret
being, while the dentist
periodically pats my arms
as if we were emerging together
from a football huddle.
He says "My wife and I went
to the Bali Hai last night,
there was almost nobody
there, it was beautiful,
the clouds and the rain.
Am I hurting you?
Rinse, please."

Meanwhile I've begun to float
on Monet's lily pond, the shrill
whir of the drill, and the slight pain,
dissolving into that much-painted

pond, into shimmering, rippling
red    blue    purple    green.

"This is the hard part, getting
the silver out.  Am I hurting you?
Thanks for being such a good patient."
More football arm-pats, and
"Rinse, please. We're half way there."

I remind my muscles to relax,
let drill and dentist dissolve,
watch them swirl away
into lily-pond pink,
yellow, lavender, blue.
At the edge of the pond,
the old man himself sits
with his easel and palette,
brush poised.

"Rinse please, there's a little silver
in there. Am I hurting you?
We're three-quarters through.
It looks good."

Monet takes my hand, tells me,
though he's painted this pond
in so many lights, so many moods,
dawn to dusk, season by season,
there's something I don't seem
to have understood: that he's been
in love with the pond, has loved it
as mother loves child, as husband
loves wife, not for its physical
beauty alone, but for its changes,
for the years of watching them,
for the way they've revealed
the pond's ineluctable being.
Painting for him has been making
love – every caress of the brush.

"Now I'm going to put a mold in.
Please bite down, that's right,
all the way down and then hold.
One minute more."

It's as if we are floating together,
the old artist and I, the lily pond
supporting our bodies, and we've
begun to make love, but he's also
painting the pond we're floating on,
and I'm making poems,
each small dab of the brush,
each vowel, each pause,
the magic of flesh warming flesh:
pleasure stretching my language
open and wet, a delicious
squishing and sliding, as words,
surrendering, allow me to receive
the gift of his dawn-to-dusk love,
his love of all seasons,
this pond loved and painted,
for all of its changes, this pond
wholly painted and loved.

"All done. Your cheek is numb, even
if it doesn't feel numb, so if you
eat a donut, be careful. Thanks
for being such a good patient."

I think of the loneliness of the dentist,
peering into mouths that can't answer,
forgetting how to listen, by necessity
engaging in one-way conversation,
while his patient eludes him,
preferring to float on a lily pond.

## Visiting Grandpa
### (1993)

You sit on your summer verandah
so mild and still that wild chickadees graze
from your palm, while I lounge, a young girl
with a book, in the neighboring lot, serenaded
by the hum and whir of insect wings, steady swoosh
of the river, the occasional train rumbling past.

One day I'll look
back to wonder
about the tall man
you might have been
if polio hadn't
shriveled your legs,
required you
like a woman
to calm and persuade
when a whole man
might bully or push.
Would Grandmother,
who watched her own
father night after night
strike her mother,
would Grandmother
have married an
uncrippled man?
Or your brothers
who helped you through
Harvard, had you been fit
to be a cabinetmaker like them,
would they have helped?
Or the newspaper columns
you wrote for forty years,
about these Berkshire Hills,
about people and places
you loved with a writer's
detail, would they
have been written?

A mile up the Deerfield river,
I now sit in the grassy curve where
"Our Hilltown Friend and Neighbor"
marks your grave. If polio hadn't taken
the spring from your step and left you,
as if in return, the hushed world of
writing, could you and I meet here
together, watching birds swoop
through this valley we love?

## It's Not as Simple as Kissing a Frog
(1992)

Here's how it is: you with your
sky blue eyes, more transparent
and startling than ever
beside the snow white
of your beard and hair,
and the way your eyes shine,
there's no doubt in my mind
that we're both in love,
as I answer the long list
of questions you've made
about the computer we gave you.

"Prince Charming," we called him:
in 1983, a state of the art IBM PC,
the year I moved in with Christine,
one year before she and I married.
We upgraded his memory then
from the original 128 to 256K;
his successors, less than a decade
later, have hard disks with 50M.
Chris and I bought two Macs
with color screens. We take for granted
nearly 400 times the memory storage,
take for granted the increase in speed.
Prince Charming, when we gave him
to you, was already a dinosaur,
yet for you he was new and strange.
It took years for you to begin to learn
word processing. You preferred to sit
at your old familiar manual typewriter,
carefully whiting out and retyping,
while Prince Charming stood idly by.

One day you bought a new computer desk
that we all assembled together. Another day
you and I bought a new desk chair.
Then you at last ventured forth
to learn, and we began weekly visits,

these question and answer sessions.
At first I thought I would scream
with impatience: you wanted to know everything
before you would touch a key, type a letter.
I've tried and tried to explain
the technical view of the world:
you don't need to understand,
you don't need to know why,
you just learn how to do things.
But you're an incorrigible humanist.
Stubbornly, you ask your unending
questions: "What does this particular
error message mean?"
"Papa, let's just do a reset, you hit
a wrong key by mistake, let's go on,"
"What does the name of each program
in the operating system mean?"
"Papa, you use them, you don't need
to know what they mean."
Carefully, like a scribe, writing down
by hand all that you learn, you make
detailed expositions of what
the manual already says.

And then something happens. You stay
curious, but you also begin to play.
I stay practical, but I begin to enjoy
the slow pools of time I'm spending with you,
the rapid ticking of my middle-aged heart
being pleasurably detained.
We both start to relish our visits.
A great blue twinkle comes into your eye.
Looking past you into the mirror
I am surprised to see a beautiful woman.
Not young anymore, but radiantly
beautiful - a smile that spreads
over her face so effortlessly,
the kind of smile that emerges only
in moments of rare carefree love.
No taut muscles propping up
the corners of the mouth, no work,

no strain, a smile held up only by joy.
I never knew how beautiful I was,
before seeing that face, illumined with love.
I look back at you, those same incredibly
blue eyes, dancing with fondness,
full of me and my beauty.

In my girlhood, they seemed remote,
those eyes, I could never quite capture
their gaze. You were busy and hurried,
an ambitious dad in middle age.
I remember when we toured Boston,
how I dawdled, wanted to discover
every detail slowly –very brick, every
bridge, every swan–slowly and in
my own time, how you made me go
at your pace, and I hated you for it.
Now it is you, in this seventy sixth
year of your life, it is you who moves
slowly, dawdles, enjoys the attention
to details. I wanted to rush you through
learning this computer as surely as you
rushed me through Boston,
yet somehow a miracle happened:
I slowed down. It's as if in my own
frantic hurry I learned to forgive
that urgent middle-aged father, in my slow
growing patience with you, I learn
to relive, to give the child I was
what she couldn't get enough of:
time just to be with you.
Looking at you
and into the mirror behind,
I see the beautiful reflection
of a woman I am learning
to love, slowly,
and in time.

## When Bubbles Burst
### (2007)

I am a young girl
and my father
is a handsome young man
with dark hair.

He stands on the Concord Bridge reciting

*By the rude bridge that arched the flood*
*their flag to April's breeze unfurled*
*here once the embattled farmers stood*
*and fired the shot heard round the world.*[1]

Years pass.
I am a woman approaching old age.
Fathers, farmers, poems, places--
nothing turned out to be simple.

Not even my white-haired father's final wish
to live and die at home
among familiar faces.

His heart's failing first.
His whole body is not,
as he always hoped,
going to end all at once
like the wonderful one-hoss shay
in the poem his father recited to him
when he was a boy.

*What do you think the parson found,*
*When he got up and stared around?*
*The poor old chaise in a heap or mound,*
*As if it had been to the mill and ground!*
*You see, of course, if you're not a dunce,*
*How it went to pieces all at once,*

---

1     *The Concord Hymn*, Ralph Waldo Emerson

*— All at once, and nothing first, —*
*Just as bubbles do when they burst.*[2]

---

2    *The Deacon's Masterpiece—or The Wonderful One-Hoss Shay*, by Oliver Wendall Holmes

# The Empty Spool

## This Breakfast Never Happened
### (1968)

This breakfast never happened.
Fancy remembers it
from my childhood home's imagined kitchen
when sunlight walked along its windowsills
unabashedly striping common things with magic
while Mother sat beside the kitchen table
and Dad with absolute tenderness
touching her hair, touching her brow.

## Ode to an Empty Spool
### (2002)

I don't remember what we children called
the empty cable spool in our backyard
but my bare toes remember
how they once hugged its center.

We practiced backward steps to make it roll,
fell often to learn balance and stand tall:
how happily we wound
our days and world around

the hollow center of that empty spool.

**One Week into the War Against Iraq – Friday March 27 2003**

Suppose you spend the day on strike from responsibility,
cooking all day because cooking is the most
comforting thing you know how to do, creative
in such a pure way: no pressure, complete
trust that whatever you do will nourish and give
pleasure no matter how imperfect your skill
and because even when nothing else can touch
the heaviness of your heart you can still
feel awe at the alchemy of the kitchen.

Take for instance
the transparency of today's air mingling with egg whites,
the beaters whirring so fast the blurred blades remind you
of hummingbird wings, and the sudden steep white rising up into peaks
above the brim of the bowl in a perfect miracle
everyday as the dawn,  leaving your heart light
as the puffed way-high-up golden brown beautiful
egg-white-only soufflé just out of the oven,
and the feeling of eating a cloud.

## The White Swan
(1973)

White swan,
you are all I rely on.
The absolute curve of your neck
your wings settled down.
Late daylight slants toward you,
bright knife-blade, bright lover.
Your boundaries waver and fade,
your substance spills over.
Light into light is scattered and gone.

Nothing can put you together.

## Now I Do Not
### (1965)

Now I do not
look up when you pass.
Only an eyelid quivers
somewhere in my
girlhood.

## After the First Collapse There Is No Other
(2001)

When the twin towers of her childhood
hurled words against one another
words huge and heavy with fuel and innocence
words ominous as jetliners piloted by terrorists

All that she knew of security
flamed up in that crash
and slowly collapsed
and slowly came tumbling down.

Below the hole in the sky
where loving parents once stood
she and her dog searched the rubble
for whatever might have survived.

If she fled into the imaginary world
of mathematics and science
where rules and logic and predictability
so soothed and amused,

She never once mistook it
for the bombed-out city
of lived experience,
where her first postulate was:

"Chaos rules,"
so that, after the first collapse,
there could be no other.

## For My Maternal Grandfather, H.L. Nunn
### (1972)

"I sing because I'm afraid," I said
sitting beside your shaggy proud head
too weak to be raised again
before your last night.
You squeezed my scared hand
tightly in your calm one.

When I think of it now,
how the dead and the dying
comfort the young
I want to grow old as you did,
solitary and mild,
a clear light upon
the darkening ocean.

## For My Sister Judy
   (1972)

We swing wide in our distinct circles
hawk-sister
sister of the wide wingspread.

Even your sweet calls
can't span the great distance
though they move like meteors, fast,
they are too vanishing.
They vanish as grandfathers do
sounds and lives alike leak through
the one small puncture in our universe.

Only the distances do not vanish
the voids that separate sister things
this nothingness that comes between us
is constant enough for measuring.

Everything else is constantly changing
everything else is vanishing
everything else–we are all of us sisters,
we the quick-passing, the children of time–
except what stays, what we can measure,
and it is no kin of mine.

# Driftwood

*For Chris*
(1983)

After the great sea storms
you bring me a gift of driftwood.
I watch it lie on my desk–it seems to want
to become the waves that have shaped it,
full of the fluid grace of your belly and thighs
when our love is in motion.

I am not home yet from my own storm.
Still dangerous, the cliffs in my mind
continue collapsing.  The elemental rage,
to my human mind so senseless,
the rage is not spent.

I carry sandbags and boulders to protect our new home.
Did we build too near to the ocean?
After the storm, will there be anything left?
I watch tall gray waves thrust their spray higher and higher
against a gray sky, and I wait.

## After the Granddaughters Leave
(2001)

After the granddaughters leave
the house breathes a vast voluminous silence,
empty of running feet, empty of sudden voices,
so like the place on my chest where the baby just slept,
where now no small heart beats near mine.

### In Celebration of the Marriage
### of Will Hamilton, forester, and Jackie Sargeson, pilot
### September 20, 1997

As serene as a bird, she crosses the sky,
her landings as soft as a breath or a sigh.
The green surge in each seedling reforests his soul,
while the angle of wind against wing makes hers soar.

Moist, deep, and green grows the heart of his dream,
like moss curtains hung from old rain forest trees.
Vast, blue and pure stretches her open gaze
like a sky undiscovered by footprints or leaves.

Two days past their wedding the Equinox, poised,
holds perfect the balance of daytime and night,
and I think of their marriage of forest and sky.

I think about trees, how freedom for trees
means to stay
in one place and to drink
the earth's life through their roots.
I think about pilots and birds,
wild creatures for whom
the sweetness of life means to move.

When I think of their marriage of forest and sky
I see a bird coming and going
among the high tops of trees
as if stitching the blue to the green,
and the tops of the trees
swaying and waving and clapping
and stretching up higher and higher
as if to catch just a moment more
of that sweet bird's sweet passing.

When I think of their marriage of forest and sky
I see trees with direction and reason
to grow and to stretch,
and I see a bird
with a place and a season
to nest.

**Melody for Marcy**

*in celebration of her birthday, January 1997*

It would be a mischievous song,
the type she might try to hide
under a bright red hat, but
it would peek out like a kitten
and purr and knead and rub,
in spite of something stately
about her, something strong
and calm you knew you could rely on,
something perfectly serious,
still it would be as if you were
children seated together in church,
hands folded on laps,
trying to be perfectly still,
trying to be very good, and then
the melody would begin to leak out
softly, in the tiniest whispers at first,
harmless little kernels of sound
that would begin to pop wildly open
until there would be an explosion of them
climbing higher than the snow of the century,
piling up past your knees, past your waist,
past your elbows, your chin, Marcy's melody
climbing clear up to your eyes,
so you couldn't help catching each other's gaze,
so you'd burst into giggles together,
which would only help further the flood
that would fill the entire church until
the walls shook, resounding with music,
and some say her melody
could be heard as far away
as Seattle, and others say, Heaven.

## Learning to Play the Cello
### (1998)

In the photo, our mother
is still alive.
She sits with her feet
planted firm on the ground,
her legs spread wide
to receive the cello
between her knees.

The long fingers of her left hand
touch the cello,
which leans into her body
like a lover.

The long fingers
of her right hand are being
positioned on the bow
by a woman conductor.

Our mother's head turns
toward her right hand,
that hand that is still
as strong and as beautiful
as it was in our childhoods.

Our mother's eyes,
infinitely attentive,
infinitely sad,
follow the bow.

You can see she has trouble
relaxing her grip.
The conductor's fingers
encircle her wrist
as if trying
to help her let go.

**The New Pink Bedroom**
*for my stepmother Jean*
(1999)

That pink bedroom you redecorated for me
without my permission
the summer I was twelve
was an invasion.

I never once thought
of the money and hours you spent
choosing the delicate pink flowered fabric
that matched so well
my grandfather's cast-off burgundy carpet.
I never counted your hours and effort
of stitching the seams, gathering ruffles,
forming and fitting bedspreads and curtains and lampshade,
painting the walls pink, the dresser white,
the drawer fronts pink, the smooth round knobs white.

All I saw was a pink trojan horse, your weapon
smuggled inside my own bedroom,
meant to burn down and destroy the walls of my city,
just another act of aggression
within the long siege of divorce.

I never once thought that for you it might
have been meant as an offering of affection.
I never thought you were trying
to build a bridge between us, to bless
my girlhood flowering into womanhood.

Forty years have gone by,
but that new pink bedroom is still just as vivid to me
as the first time I saw it.
I no longer recall how the room looked before.

I know now the courage and strength
that it must have taken for you

even to try to break a trail through the thorns
that surrounded the heart of that hurt angry child.

Across forty years, I send back my thanks.

**For Kandis**

*Orcas Island artist, tea ceremony master, and hairdresser*
(1999)

For she is the master of a ceremony
more ancient than tea.

And sacred is the way in which
she washes and touches a woman's head.

And sacred what she knows when she touches
wet hair, alive and growing between her fingertips.

And sacred the moment
when she lifts up her scissors to trim.

And sacred the gaze of each woman
into the mirror that Kandis holds

Beyond the face that she thinks that she knows
to the face  - changing, radiant, strange - that is her soul's.

**Melinda, Deborah, Ailia**
   *Orcas Island midwife, mother, daughter*
   (1999)

Melinda comes to Ailia's birth directly from dancing,
in her veils and bracelets of a belly dancer,
knowing Deborah well, knowing a little bare belly and spangle
will not distract Deborah from the business at hand,
the serious business (for which belly dancing is merely

the ritual practice), the serious business
of Deborah slipping herself delicately through the contractions,
as a wrist slips itself through an endless succession of bracelets.
The serious, sacred business of parting the veils between the worlds,
the serious drumbeat dance of Deborah's belly against the new life,

the serious dance of the hands and feet and emerging head
of the infant Ailia,
for whom Melinda's braceleted arms and bare belly
form the first welcome: a dancer's welcome to this child, who,
years later, grown into a dancer too, now swings
round the Orcas Community Center stage with her midwife Melinda.

Ailia's grown woman's hips roll and toss,
her grown woman's lips curve into a smile.

## Voice of the Aborted Child
   *for Linda*
   (1979)

So that you could live, I died.
It wasn't time for a physical child.

I leapt, little fish, out of womb into dream,
vast ocean of green where I swam
through a gold undulation of leaves,
stately sea forest, out of whose shadows
ancient eyes beamed, blue, yellow, orange.

I whispered sea secrets into your soft silences,
vast possibilities, hidden treasures,
long-sunken ships, trunks of gold coin
clasped in the slow embrace of wild coral.

Hearing my voice, you learned how to sing.

Now in the clamor of cigarettes, alcohol, pills,
wrapped in small dreams of numb death,
you don't listen.

Mother, I whisper vast dreams, vast dreams
            into your heart.
I died so you could live them.
I died—do you hear me?—I died,
so you could live them.

You, warrior woman. You, with the hidden
invisible strength, I'm talking to you.
Now listen.
It isn't time to abort me now.
Now is the time to fight.

## Abortion

*for Kaaren*
(1972)

Bishops and lawyers, my love,
debate your soul
whose bellies are empty.

My heart hears yours
like a soft echo, my warm belly
surrounds you like a glove.
We know what they don't know—
how to live in one body.

Inside I love you fiercely.
Outside I am numb.
Outside I have failed.
I found no place for you.

There isn't space for you.
I'll have to kill one of us.

## Womb-Crying
*for Kaaren*
(1972)

Kaaren,
tonight I solved the puzzle–
you're my daughter.
Where I feel you is inside.
A month past your abortion
I'm still bleeding
(womb-crying, as you said).

But not for what's been done.
Fresh loss, fresh blood.

I know I can't have you
or hold you or touch you.
I love you.
You have have turned me
inside out
like a mother.

Kaaren, no one,
no one in all the world,
feels anything more delicate than I do–
the pain of your growing
faster than I am.

## The Planter

*for my brother Scott—and for his son Elliot who at three years old said "I'm a pottery man like my Dad. I'm an art man, and I'm totally out of control."*
(1992)

Like most of your vases,
it's Celadon-glazed,
white barely hinting at green,
fragile and young as morning mist,
egg of a vanishing bird.

As always your etched designs are delicate,
and I picture your huge bear body
bent, great paw clasping some tiny
implement, slowly carving the shape
of a womb, the curved child inside
from whose open fingers spill seed
into the mothering ground, the womb
swirling up into petaled labia, out of which
a stalk rises, bearing an ear of new corn,
silk waving, husk splitting to show
row after row of ripening seed.

My eyes slide over the smooth form
of this vase, as I think of you, three
when our mother left, three
when our father withdrew into work,
eight and nine when two sisters,
one of them me, also deserted.
I think of your wife, tired
of how little you earn with your art
while you stay with your three year old son.

I wonder where it comes from,
love that survives so much loss.
I think of the sister who never left,
who showed me this vase, your thanks
for a weekend she stayed with your son
during the long barren years of waiting
for her own child to come.

### Seventy-Seventh Birthday
### (1993)

Not just the deafness and peoples' voices drifting away,
not just my children moving to different cities,
but my own bones and muscles refusing
to move as freely, narrowing
the circumference of my
day. Seventy-seven
was the year the
world began
to shrink.

# THE PHILIP POEMS

## Portrait of Philip on his Fortieth Birthday
January 25, 1983

The fluttering raven, frightened now, breaking free from the back of your head, its dark gleaming feathers, wide open beak, wild call, terrified talons, spread wings. The fluttering fear behind your eyes which see deeper into me than I dare to be seen. The dark distances behind your eyes, the raven fluttering, the back of your mind backing into desperation. To be so seen terrifies, in such contrast to your warm surface, the crinkled edges that still cannot cancel the black holes in the eyes, the dark centers through which the fluttering raven's scream can almost be heard. And if I should fall into those eyes, to the back where even now I feel the raven straining to escape, would I not be pounded thin as the wind by those wings?

You, beautiful as a fairy tale prince, man-boy at forty beginning the central quest even now in your own dark woods, Dantean, deep in the middle of the middle of your life, wandering far from your origins, still far also from your circling back, only by the pure light that comes from the other prince will you find your way back. His hand even now extends, offers you a goblet of water and light. This blond prince who braves your dark woods, the night eyes of your animals on him, who enters the holes in your eyes, who does not fear the raven, who holds out the pure cup of light, who meets you where no one else has dared come. This is the Meeting of your life. To receive the cup, to release the prince, to allow this meeting - the kiss of his fair quest, your dark quest - to accomplish its meaning. The prince who must go leaves you alone to face your danger, the raven wings beat louder and louder, as you drink deeply, the sound of them deafening, as you drink deeply, the raven breaking free, as you drink deeply, tearing a whole in the back of your head, as you drink deeply, suddenly, sunlight is streaming in. The edge of your woods has been reached.

The raven is free. I am not afraid anymore to be seen, even as deeply as you can see. Behind the holes in your eyes, I see you circling. Solid ground, a calm meadow.

## Dear Philip
  (1991)

An emotion is not enough
to make a poem. Especially
an emotion like this one,
tongue stuck in my
gullet, inarticulate,
a companion ache
in my lungs as I think
of the fungus
shadowing yours.
"Bronchoscopy" -
a sense of violation
in my throat as I imagine
that necessary yet forced
insertion,
or the new catheter,
semi-permanent,
intruder perpetually
piercing your skin.

The borders between you
and the world are not intact.
The slow trek toward your
much too imminent death
has begun. I think you will
go on fighting. I think there is hope
in you vast and immovable
as a mountain. But you and I
both know the darkness.
You could have been my brother.
I could have stood with you
as a child, my small hand in yours,
gazing together into
the unfathomable depths
of the world's deepest canyon.
We know how far down
one can look.

78

And then there's my lover.
She who has taught me
the mystery of safety:
feeling loved.
You left her, called by
the truth of your flesh to find
a love wholly consecrated
by your body, you left her
to me.

The first time she introduced us,
you brought flowers, blessed
our fledgling love, told me how
beautiful I was, made me feel
I deserved to love and be loved.

Now I am powerless to ease one
step of your path.
Each moment that I live pain-free,
free of the shadow of death,
surrounded by love - that sacred
illusion of safety - may I bring part
of you with me, away from all
pain, away from all fear,
away from all violation.
As you walk your almost
impossible path, know that you
have planted seeds in me, know
that they will do honor to you,
know they will go on
flowering.

Love, River

## I Imagine The Wedding
### (1992)

At the edge of the canyon, a
shivering crowd. Under the tent
fortuitously raised just in case
of this rain, which does pour, well-
wishers huddle. And you, pale and
thin and gray as a very old
man, are giving your daughter
a blessing: watching her wed
the man she has chosen,
while death clings to you,
like a greedy infant guzzling
down your frail life.

Yet you're here, the Philip we
know, struggling against the
undertow of your disintegrating
body to be for this one moment
whole. There's little left now
of personal will, only the need to
soothe through this transition
those who rely on you, until
you must go, leaving them
nothing but your utterly unconsoling
absence for which precisely because
of how generously you succor,
neither you nor they are prepared.

**Philip Fades**
    (1992)

He grows grayer
and more skeletal,
though he glows
remarkably
with the haunting
memory of his
former beauty.
Even strangers
can see it.
Gazing at him,
it's as if
I stand by
watching vandals
hammer away
at Michelangelo's David.

## Visiting Philip, June, 1992

How strange to see you, Philip,
changed by illness at last into
someone I barely recognize,
more like a picture from a
magazine, an anonymous victim
of AIDS or of famine, than
your own particular person:
the same hollow cheeks, the
same angular legs, your skin
abandoned by flesh, cringing
against uncushioned bones.

Before this, you'd always slip on
long ample pants, a fresh shirt,
dazzling blue - perhaps one we'd
given to you - fool us into seeing
the beautiful man you once were.

Now you wear shorts, bland shirt,
chin stubbled grey, as if to concede
you can't masquerade, not today.

Yet as soon as you speak of your
children, your eyes sparkle, and
beautiful Philip shines through.

You tell how Ryan helps you to the
bathroom when you can't walk alone,
how Kyle gives you a bicycle horn
for Father's Day, to rouse her out
of deep sleep, as neither your cry,
nor the loud clanging of a bell,
have been able to do.

For yourself, you might rather
be dead. For your children, you
live, hoping this hard work of
helping reveals to them the sinew
and muscle of love, the toughness

you never required of them, which
they'll need when you're gone.

## The Day Philip Died
   (1992)

It was if we two sat silent,
there at the pond's edge, air
throbbing with secrets. A
Mayfly paused on your wrist.
My eye hovered near your eye,
lingered on wings thin as the
edge of a breath, green as
spring shoots, pale as death.

We traced the riddle of veins
through motionless wings,
transparent as light.

Then the Mayfly flew,
and the night in your eyes
huddled like a child against
the night in my eyes.

**For Caroline**
    (1991)

I think of you often
your body naked
in a plain pine
box
slowly
resolving itself
into the simple
elements
from which it
came.

3 am.
The hour empty
as a cradle
and calling
your name.

The strange silence
awaiting the breath
that will not
be breathed.
The strange silence
between
your life ending
and mine
continuing.

Your hand in mine,
your fingers and forearm
stiffening.

When I let go,
your gesture is permanent,
a sculpted relief
of our two hands
holding:
your arm lifted,

your fingers curved
around empty space.

I would have liked
to go with you,
holding your hand,
stepped through the dark
threshold together,
a brave big sister
calming your fears,
pretending
I know the way
to the promised land.

## Made to Exist
(2006)

That we begin at last
to grasp the pathos
of a white table
made to exist
so close to the sea
but never to swim or to sail
and then the tender possibility
of a baby goat standing
apart from its mother
on a cliff near the Cretan sea
still eyeing the world
with curiosity that does not
know how to distinguish
the scent of a foe from a friend
but for us who sit naked
on the deeper blue
of this blanket
never to be mistaken for
that blurring of blues
where sea and sky meet
losing themselves forever
or perhaps only failing
to find themselves
in each other –
I sit here
in the accurate rhythm
of your sleeping breath
and only the shower
that has forgotten the hour of
its flowing and will not
remember until
the touch of my hand to
your breast yes there are
impossibilities that unfold
every moment
each wave of your breath
rises through the broken
dispersing foam of the last

we are dying
creatures at best
but please
go on breathing
asleep at my side, now
that we've lived intertwined
long enough to know
love is not that youthful
delirious desire
or not that alone
love slowly ages
becomes
the slowness of your
sleeping breath
the possibility of
eyes meeting across
the impossible breach
between your life
and mine
each breath rising
through the brokenness
of the last–
love itself, Aphrodite,
the tearing foam lace
of your birth
the dying wave
out of which
the new one rises yes
as if we knew anything then
about what love now is
instead we become
a white table
made to exist
so close to the sea
which to sail or to swim
is not our destiny.

## The Goodbye
   (1995)

This morning, Mother, I strolled with my
friend Janet down the incline to the ferry,
carrying her bag, hugging a slow goodbye,
letting our lips brush
                    slightly
                              (not to risk having
our flesh recall one night ten years ago when we
yielded to the moon pull, tides of two oceans
perilously rising together, not now when we
are solidly friends, grateful for stable ground
under our feet: just think how in California
the solidest ground has been bucking and shaking
so no one - not even a surfer - feels quite at home).

We arrive early, share a slow breakfast
at the Orcas hotel, aroma of coffee, flaking
of biscuits, omelets bulging with sprouts,
scallions, tomatoes; potatoes pan-fried crisp
golden brown. From our window, a view
through the garden, sun spilling among tall
hollyhocks, roses, poppies, down to the landing,
the silent ferry emerging from behind hills,
between islands, moving to Shaw first,
stopping, steering toward Orcas, bountiful
time to gather and lift Janet's bags, to stroll
to the landing, bask in warm sun, hug one
another precisely, with care, and release
all we can be to each other, all we cannot be.

I leave, sparkle of sunshine on water, through
trees, percolating my mood like good coffee,
as I recall my last trip to this ferry. Early morning,
December chill on the air, racing the car, thinking
*we're late, we won't get there, we'll miss the ferry,*
*she'll miss her plane,* you with your difficult
ankle trying to run, clumsy with weight of suitcases,
adrenaline gripping my heart, the palpable guilt, then
they raise the barrier for you, and you disappear.

I'm left with the lack of goodbye, our visit
unblessed, unraveling like the fogged day.

This longing for everything precious to finish
in beauty, as on a sunny day. In a poem, in
life, things don't always end that way.

# What We Think We Have Wasted

## Postcard from Vienna
   (1991)

A few hours after we talked on the phone,
you walked to Bergasse 19–thinking
of the professor who shaped your life and mine,
who taught us to honor the unattainable,
and then to renounce it with love, to domesticate
our wild longings into incomplete, civilized lives.
His memory even now holds our love in his
careful hands as if we were among his most
precious objects, as if in that consulting room,
so respectful of the innocent beasts that hide
under our civilized skins, he collected
artifacts of the future, as well as the past.

How moving for you to walk up the stairs
so many have climbed, their memoirs
still footsteps within your mind, only to find
the furniture vanished: his couch, the birthing
rug, the hardwood glass cases of books,
the gods and goddesses–gone. Gone to
London to flee the jaws of those all too
human dangers he helped so many to tame.
You were glad that we'd gone there together,
to London, where his treasures found shelter
against all that still prowls.

In the postcard, an aging Freud, perfectly
groomed–polished shoes, tailored suit,
trimmed moustache and beard, thinning
white hair, spectacles–sits beside a
large bowl of fruit, embracing a dog.

## The Caged Bear

> *SARAJEVO, Bosnia and Herzegovina, Oct. 15, 1991 – The*
> *animal house at the Sarajevo zoo is almost silent now, except for*
> *volleys of automatic rifle fire directed toward it from the heights*
> *immediately above. . . .Only one animal, a female black bear,*
> *remains alive of the 100 there when the siege began in April.*
> *– John Burns, The New York Times*

All my life I have lived in this small locked cage
looking out through bars at your species, pondering
strangers who captured my ancestors, not to fill
empty bellies, not to clothe shivering skin,
not to taste the ecstasy of the kill, but to make
a display so their children can stare, pointing and
laughing, while I defecate, urinate, scratch,
or lie down. By now I know more about you
than I care to, while, exiled from bear world
and ways, I have no one to teach me who bear
really was, only my dreams to tease me with
hints of lost being. Your stories and science
know more about me than I do. My grandmother
lacked words; she needed bear ways to convey
her knowledge of who we once were.

Indifferently, I watch this war. Not that I'm free
of hunger or fear: I feel as you do, cramp in the gut,
weakness of vanishing muscle. I hear the explosion,
the scream of the dying or maimed. I smell the decay,
and I know the ravenous need that forced me to feed
on my brothers, sole companions of my cage.

But you know what it means to be human: far more
than the cunning to cage and display other beings.
In honor of that knowing, Suad Osmanovic,
Adem Hodzic, you two young men each
cross the hundred yards of Serbian snipers
to bring me a loaf of scarce bread. Because
I am innocent and helpless, you risk death,
not to save me, so little inclined toward saving,
but to show you still know, even in this extremity,
what the ancestors taught: you know what it means

to be human. If I knew what it means to be bear,
I too might care what will be destroyed in this war.

## A Mother at Wounded Knee
### (1992)

It's a good day to die, we have
danced the white man away
with our most sacred of dances,
we have danced the return
of the thundering buffalo herd.
Do not be afraid, my son,
though our victory is not in this
world, though this is not
the pounding of the first hooves
of the buffalo crossing back
into this world, this is not
those great beings taking
shimmering shape in the distance,
oh no, this is the cavalry coming,
their swords and guns drawn to
strike down our faith. My child,
there must come a day for
facing our death, and this is
an honorable day. We have danced
well, and the spirit has chosen
instead for us to cross over–
who knows?–to where perhaps
even now our buffalo friends may be
dancing on our behalf, dancing
to deliver us from the terrible
void in the white man's heart. When
pain comes, my son, remember
you are a young warrior,
pain will pass soon enough.
Think not about pain, think how
you and I will soon be together,
how we will see the great buffalo
brothers come thundering down
the beautiful, unravished plain.

## A Mother at Dachau
(1992)

God, if you had given me only
the blue of the summer sky,
it would have been enough.
If you had given me only
the sparkling brook of my
mother's laughter, it would
have been enough. If you had
given me only the juice of my
husband's body sweating and
surging into mine,
it would have been enough.
If you had given me only
the first flutter of life
inside my own womb,
it would have been enough.
If you had given me only
the first look into my daughter's
clear eyes, it would have been
enough. If you had given me
only the strength to be calm,
to hold my child in love, clear
through to the end, it would
have been enough.

But God, you do not abandon me,
even in this foul place, you come,
you are willing to stay, you have
not turned your face away, though
you weep and tremble just as mortal
fathers do, who know, bone thin and weak
as they are, that they cannot protect
their own children. You stay–you who
could go–stay, promising me that
our people will live, will fill the
earth as the stars fill the sky. We will
give birth, sing, have our high holidays. This
dream of fear will not end our story.

## The Slaveowner's Child
### (1992)

At ninety-seven my grandfather knew
that *nigrahs* were not, as he had been
taught, simple lovable creatures in need
of control by the superior race.
As an infant and child, his closest adult
companion was Ma'm Mary, the former
slave who stayed on with his family,
and whom he loved dearly, just as I loved
the creature friends of my childhood,
the dog and the horse whose mute
ancient gaze taught me more about love
than human beings could, with the sharp
shining edge of their words.
      (For years I wanted to write
a poem soft as those animal eyes, but somehow
the poetry stiffened almost as soon as I
poured it into words, as if the real poetry
rode on the wind that blew through their eyes,
as if the real poetry hovered on the updrafts
of silence, could not be made captive of words.)

Those animal friends, in their way, had also
been slaves, yet I seemed to find in their eyes
a freedom lost to the master race.

At ninety-seven my grandfather knew
that Ma'm Mary too should have shared
in his birthright: dominion over the earth,
the plants, the animals, over all the world
beneath his high hierarchical forehead,
the world without the crowning gift of
consciousness, the crowning sword of words.
Before he died he spoke to her, from his world
of the living, he spoke through to her world
of the dead, to the very woman who almost
a century before had cradled his naked
newborn body, had lifted the ample purple
of her nipple to his pink pale lip, yet who as he grew

called him "Sir," and all the while, his deepest,
darkest, most secret memories of love smelled
like her. "Ma'm Mary," my grandfather
said, "can you forgive me for not knowing
that you also were human?"
Ma'm Mary's laugh was molasses as she strolled
through the lilacs of heaven eternally blooming.
"Child," she said, "can you forgive me
for not knowing that you were a slave?"

## The Day of the Dead

*for Kornelia, October 29, 1991*

*This sentiment moves all survivors; they owe nothing to anyone
but everything to the dead…Why do I write? To wrench those
victims from oblivion. To help the dead vanquish death.—Elie
Wiesel*

In Mexico, on the Day of the Dead,
the entire village makes a parade,
laden with baskets, into the burial grounds.
There they spread open their blankets
and picnic over their family graves.
With the bones of the dead below them,
the living break bread, and the bread that
they break is baked in the shape of skulls.

In Greece, Orthodox Christians bury
food with their dead–an ancient pilaf
of barley, sesame, wheat, combined
with blood-red seeds of the pomegranate.
Within the open casket, the once living body
lies motionless, cold, while the living gaze
at their dead one final time, gathering
to partake of the same grains and seeds
that garnish the corpse. Generations
before Jesus Christ through whose
body and blood these Greeks still partake
of their dead and resurrected Lord–
their ancestors made pilgrimage
to the secret mysteries of Eleusis,
perhaps to partake of Demeter, goddess
of grains and all things that grow,
and her lost and risen daughter
Persephone who, having been abducted
by Hades, grim king of the world below,
and having tasted the ruby red seeds
of the dead, could be freed each year
to return only in spring.

You, Kornelia, remember your
country, Hungary before the war,

seen through a child's eyes.
How the whole country was Catholic
and on All Saints Day everyone poured
out into the streets, stuffing the trolleys
with people, chrysanthemums–
white and yellow bouquets, wreathes,
blossoms, petals everywhere,
people venturing forth to the graveyards,
honoring their dead. Too young to mourn
for the dead, you rejoiced in the holiday,
your whole country doing the same
thing together, the shared parade.

It was years before you noticed the others,
those who had not marched in the Catholic
parade. Yellow stars marked their houses.
They were your best friend, your neighbor,
your teacher, the people your country was unable
to defend. They became your dead, but left
no marked graves to carry chrysanthemums to,
and in any case how could you celebrate them
with a ritual they died for not sharing?

Later, walking the ruined streets of Budapest,
piled with rubble deeper than the entire
height of a door, you dreamed of rebuilding,
of houses where young married couples
could live, apart from the weight
of the last generation. But it was the dead,
not only the young, you dreamed of sheltering.
For you had taken them in, you
carried them with you wherever
you went. They had no other grave.

## Torrey Pine
### (1992)


Down canyon from my writing cabin, you stand–
tall and solid as the imagined father of my girlhood,
seemingly invincible, your quiver of needles
dispersing green-silver into the wind-ruffled day.
Your vigorous boughs almost imperceptibly swing
and sway, and my window is full of you, even
with your head and feet outside my view.

How does it feel, Torrey Pine, to be a survivor?
So many of your kind have died, gasping
to breathe the smogged air, groping
to find water in the drought-plagued earth,
so exhausted they fall easy prey to insects
which all but the weakest used to resist,
so that now the park bearing your name
has become a ghost forest, rattling
with the rust-colored bones of dead trees.

When I was a child and my mother had left,
a distant relative of yours, a juniper shrub
whom I thought was a tree, took me in. She let
me enter into the cool green curved cave
under her lowest limb and there she soothed
and cradled and sang to me, lent sap and root
and even the green leaf mystery to me, not
caring how foreign the species from which
I came, simply knowing that I was at risk,
knowing that we living things are together in this.

I would in her memory hold you, Torrey Pine,
in these human arms, would comfort and cradle,
bend finger, voice, tongue–and perhaps even
now this poem will slip through the glass pane
of my window, this voice will wrap itself gently
around and surround you, so that you can know
in each needle, each branch, and each cone,
how I hold you within the mystery of my

human mind, so that you can know, oh tree
of a dying tribe, that you are not alone.

## Lover's Gift

*You only need to let the soft animal of your body*
*love what it loves.—Mary Oliver*
(1993)

When I look at Tommy, the graceful gold
of his ten-year-old feline body, when I receive
in my lap his warm weight, when my flesh
echoes his purrs, I think
of the animal I might have been.

When I wake in the night to his cry
like a baby's, I know his is not
the voice of the human child
I once ached to birth.
I know he is Tommy the cat.
Nor does he cry anymore
for the long-lost breast
of the mother who nursed him
until in a swirl of tooth and claw
she banished him from her body.
He cries for the struggling warm flesh
of a captive gray mouse or brown bird
that has just now grown still,
closing the door on his rapture.
His infant cry pounds on the night,
as if need could shake the beloved awake.

When in daylight he offers
the lifeless limp flesh of his prey,
though I remove the remains
delicately in a plastic bag,
I do not undervalue the gift –
blood unsipped, flesh untasted,
passion unconsummated – I do not
undervalue the gift of this animal's love.

Still, I think of the animal I might have been,
softly purring, softly stalking, softly killing,
never knowing, oh my humankind,
how much too much I also love.

## There Are No Innocent Victims
(1992)

We have all been
the snake at the breast
the young sucking blood
from it's mother's womb,
sucking milk drawn from blood
from her chest. We have been
the cannibal-young, fed
on our mother's flesh.

There are no innocents here.
Life feeds upon life,
we have all drunk
from her blood. Not one of us
has refused the sacrifice;
giant leech upon her body,
we have all sucked
and grown strong.

Fed, sheltered, clothed
by those whose strain
on our behalf bent them
toward death, we have all
sucked at the sweet shoot of life,
that sugarcane of our parents'
marrow and bone.

Not one of us
has refused the sacrifice—
life feeding on life—
we have all been fed,
we shall all be fed upon.

## Coyote Saint Francis

*inspired by a sculpture by David Densmore*
(1999)

Just who does he think that he is,
this Coyote Saint Francis?
Does he think that he comes
from the new world, or the old?
The long-stemmed red rose
that he holds in both hands like a bludgeon
is the biggest riddle:

Its thorn-studded stem
has the burly look of a bouncer
that could evict
pleasure from paradise,
but the soft red lips of its petals promise kisses
that could lift a princess
out of thousands of years of mute sleep.

Just who does he think that he is,
this trickster Saint Francis?
The songbird perched on his shoulder
seems to be serenading a saint
as his sharp nose and ears search the air
with Coyote's own keen devotion
to greed.

**Famine**
        (1991)

On the other side of the photograph
a child is starving. Elongated fetus,
angled legs bent, thin skin draped
over bones unencumbered by flesh. Implacable
ancient eyes gaze as if through a vast expanse.
They do not beg. They do not ask.

On this side of the photograph, stomach
wresting, wringing, wrenching at the sight,
a woman buys the exhibit book, as if
it could magically soothe her anguish away.
If she wrote more checks, would it go away?
If she abstained from restaurant dinners,
movies, theatre, ceased to buy any but the most
necessary clothes, sacrificed the beauties of home,
the safety of neighborhood, responded to each
of the avalanche of mail and calls soliciting money,
would it die away? Would she be like Saint Francis and free?
Could she reach out, through the photograph,
to touch the child on the other side, the starving
child who asks nothing of anyone? Might he
light on her shoulder like a bird,
and teach her his language?

## A Bird in the Hand

*inspired by a sculpture by David Densmore*
(1991)

The hand is faithful: fingers calm,
bones sturdy, muscles and sinews strong.
At the tip of its fingers, a bird
delicate as an insect
thrums her wings,
as her throat and her beak pour forth song.
The hand has fallen in love with the bird,
it offers her refuge and shore,
while air currents drift
around and around, lift
the feathered tips of her wings, whisper
of boundless, vast, and shelterless things,
of the inconstant blue, the unfathomable black.
She will fly, and the hand cannot know
whether she will ever come back.

## Crow at the Dump
(2000)

Crow swaggers the way
the little blindfolded boy swaggers
as he swings his bat at his birthday piñata.

We do not know where
what we think we have wasted
will go, or be used, or by whom.

We only know the blue-black gleam
of crow as he contemplates
the great mound of our garbage.

## Raven
(2000)

Let's say you start out as some sort of a winged spirit
and you think you know where the secret of life is hidden
and you want to steal it, so you disguise yourself as a drink
of water and you slip through the lips, through the throat,
of an old man's beautiful daughter, and you hide yourself there
deep down inside her, where you grow and you grow
and you take on the shape of a girl or a boy,
let's say it's your choice, and you're born.

And you warm the old man completely
with the fire of your laughter and the spark in your eye.
And let's say that you're longing to play
with the old man's antique collection
of nested boxes. And maybe you don't remember
exactly what secret is hidden away
inside of those boxes, but you do know
that you want to get in there,
that somehow you need to play
with those boxes, you need to be free
to open and play with precisely those boxes,
you know with all your heart and with all your soul
that you need to play with those boxes
and when he says no
you cry and you cry and you cry and will not be comforted
until something hard in him melts
and he lets you open and play with the first,
the outermost box, and for a time
you're content in your play,
and he basks in your chortles and gurgles.

Until the time comes when you need the next box,
the one that is just a little bit smaller, you need
to open and play with that next box
you know with all your heart and with all your soul,
that you need to play with precisely and only that box
and when he says no,
you cry and you cry and you cry and will not be comforted
until something hard in him melts

110

and he lets you play with the next largest box.

And so it goes, you make your hero's
journey on the sea of play, through the labyrinth
of your grandfather's boxes, until you find your destiny,
in the smallest, the ultimate box, in which,
though you may not remember
what secret first lured you into this world,
you find that as you steal it
you are transformed
into winged spirit again, you seize the secret
in the beak of your new shape of being,
spreading your unfamiliar wings out and sweeping yourself
up on the wild upward surge and convection of smoke and of spark
from the fire in the center of his house,
as he finds out that he's been betrayed,
sweeping yourself up on the surge of his fury and grief,
up through the smoke hole, out through the top of his house.

Let's say you are coated black by the ash of that smoke
and become the Raven we know, the black-winged
trickster thief, and as you sweep up with the secret you stole,
Grandfather Eagle, a spirit much older than you,
sweeps down from the sky and crashes against you,
so the secret is knocked right out of your beak,
and instantly shatters and scatters
into hundreds of billions of stars, and among them
one sun, one moon, and one earth.

How could you know,
when your trickster nature called out to you
and you sleuthed your way through the beautiful body
of an old man's daughter
into the innermost box of his soul,
how could you know
what orbits and evolutions
your curiosity would unfurl?

## Stranger
(2001)

Most mysterious stranger, you
who were so in love with possibilities
that you threw your serene unbeing
into the emptiness and broke apart
into billions of galaxies, now you burn
in my cells, in the stars, in this stone.

When I am most alone,
I can hear the shards of you moan
of their loneliness to me.
When I am most broken.
I resonate most with your song.

I know that the lure of possibilities
that persuaded you to leave the sweet
equanimity of nonbeing included
this tree, this street lamp, and me,
a woman walking on a sidewalk
strewn with dry eucalyptus leaves
under a crescent moon.

**Learning from the Masters**
   (1993)

Japanese gardeners who pick
aphids by hand, no pesticide,
hour after hour, day after day,
year after year; chimpanzees
who run long fingers
through each other's hair,
searching for fleas, ticks, mites
crunching them thoughtfully
between teeth;  you, my longtime
dog friend, who stand
silent and still while I comb
the russet silk of your hair,
catching each gleam
of black speed, freezing
it between thumb and comb,
sliding it down to soapy water,
wiping thumb and fingertip
dry, continuing to comb;
and these fleas, their generous
numbers always replenishing
like the sea, leaping like salmon
upstream toward the warm
taste of blood, remind me that
I am a servant required to stoop,
comb, and pluck, not to command.

## Molly's Goodbye

*Communicated by Molly on the last day of her life, lying with*
*her head on River's lap*
(1998)

It is time to go, River. I am going.

When, in the darkness of early dawn, you come to wake me for our morning walk, I will say "Molly is not here!" River, I am going.

I will become the slight movement of air rubbing against you, and I will become the water splashing you in the shower.

In the fall, when the golden maple leaves shine on the trail, you will feel the air stir at the wave of my invisible tail. You will see the leaves lift as I plunge my invisible nose into their sweet smell.

And when you walk swiftly up a steep path, I will be there beside you, young again, prancing, drinking in the crisp air. With your every breath, you will breathe in my love and my joy, because I will be in the autumn air all around you.

And when 5 o'clock comes, you will feel my nose nudging your hand, you will hear my imperious bark, so that you can recall it is you I depend on. Only now you will scoop out only the food of your love, and only my spirit will gobble it up.

But most of all, I will always be with you. You will never need to leave me at home. My eyes will never fill with the sadness of saying goodbye to you. When you pack a suitcase, I will not need to climb into the car to be sure I go with you. Wherever you are, I will be. Mostly I will sleep quietly there, unobtrusively at your feet. Just as it has always been, it will be enough for me simply to be in the same room with you.

And when the winter snow comes, and you walk through the ice and the snow and the harsh winds, I will be there and no ice will form between my toe pads. I will be there, taking up great mouthfuls of snow and swallowing some and tossing some up into the air, and you will be happy simply to be alive, because I always will be there.

And when it is spring, and the tiny wildflowers sing, and the fern forest recreates itself shoulder high out of nothing, I will be there with you, dancing down the path, and I will not need a leash, and I will run after the deer without ever frightening them, and without ever leaving your side.

And when it is summer, I will be in the hum of the insects and the sparkle of dragonfly wings, and when you sit very still in the summer sun, you will feel my warm body softly relaxing beside you.

And when you reach down to stroke my head, and to stroke underneath my chin and throat, I will sigh so softly you will think it is only the breeze, and I will lick your hand gently with my invisible tongue.

And when the summer subsides, and the time of my death comes around once again, I will come to you wagging my tail, valiantly loving my life, circling the lake, climbing the mountain, surpassing the capability of my failing body, and I will teach you again and again how precious life is, and how death too is a precious mysterious thing.

When you touch the big tumor that swells in my narrow body, I will teach you to touch it with love. My body will remind you of the beauty of Picasso's pregnant goat, my distended belly no less beautiful than a melon ripening in the sun. Every year I will remind you that death is a miracle too, death is a beautiful thing, just as life is. My death every year will become another gift that we give to each other as friends, another transformation of our love.

And when you miss me, I will be with you then, to comfort your sadness. And when you are able to move on, and to pour your love into the world of the living, I will be everywhere your love turns, greeting you with my wagging red tail and my brown eyes soft with love.

If you lash out at someone you love, and the violence of your own need to control causes both of you pain, I will be there with my hurt puppy eyes full of love, helping you learn all over again that love is more precious than your need for control, helping you know that you are already forgiven, that the important thing now is to grow.

And when someone asks you, "Where has Molly gone?" you will tell them "Right here, right now, Molly is in my body and in my soul, she is in the pupils of my eyes, she is in the dance of the seasons, the rhythm of the days."

## Looking for My First Kitten
   (1993)

Before I met you, what
were you doing? Walking the sky,
lapping the Milky Way? Is that why
your fur crackles with night,
your paws trail moonlight,
stars smear your face?
Is that why the green
of another world invites
through your eyes? Why the waves
of your pleasure rub against mine
until even the lack in me
stretches and purrs?

When you leave me, what
will I do? Decades after you go,
my dreams will still circle
the childhood block,
looking for you.

**Early Morning Mist**
    (1978)

Early morning mist drifts on the mountain.
The sun goes higher.
The mist lifts and vanishes.

I don't want it to go.
Somewhere in the mist
is something I need to know.

The sun also has a journey.
It can't stop or slow
to make things convenient for me.

I learn to read the signs.
There may be another morning like this,
and I will be ready.

Up before dawn in the mountains, walking,
the dissolving fingers of the tender mist talking
to my seemingly substantial body.

# FIVE LOVE SONNETS
   (1992)

## If Like My Own Flesh

If like my own flesh yours has not been touched
by a physical love wild and tenacious enough to rip
free from your pectorals, vertebrae, ligaments
the ancient artifacts of rape, the relics of hate,

then you can be my cellmate, you can slip into my side
in this shared prison of bones, to plot our escape, how
we two this moment whispering might patiently rub
word against tongue, word against rib, word against thumb,

until we both spark, until we both flame, until Santa Ana herself,
woman of wind in full heat, enters our lungs, licks each sweet
crevice of our skin, until the Mississippi in our blood rises

to full flood, shakes her hair of snakes, laughing out loud,
rampages through the museum, sweeps away hate
like dry leaves, baptizes us deep in her rich alluvial mud.

## If You Have Ever Doubted

If you have ever doubted that you are wholly loved and wanted
on this earth, choose tonight as your moment of knowing.
Open the door, step outside, feel the wind rub her cool
body against the warm firmness of yours. You can almost

feel her purr with the satisfaction of pouring herself
into each caress, leaning into the curves of your shoulders,
your throat. When you breathe, feel her slip into your nostrils,
glide down your windpipe, dart her tongue among the petals

of your lungs, delicate tissues that tremble under her touch
like sea creatures in the currents of a submerged world.
Feel her leap, a school of mermaids swimming the tides

of your blood, impressing upon each industrious cell the bare
breasts, arms, belly of her pleasure. Somewhere between your
thighs, the wind's kiss arrives, dripping: half woman, half fish.

**You Are Not Yet Persuaded?**

You are not yet persuaded? Then think of your shadow,
this patina of black attached at your feet, this brush
stroking the face of the world with its dark
mimicry of your shape. Has the ground

where you walked ever once
shrugged off your embrace, this shadow
forever falling into its arms, sighing,
substanceless, yearning for weight?

Has a wall or a sidewalk or street, however unknown
and uncourted, ever once recoiled from the dark
reflection pressing suddenly in on its sleep?

Doesn't the ground rather cling to your shadow, inert
substance craving the startle of life, as you pass by,
all knees and elbows, successes and failures, surprise.

## When Hateful Thoughts Hold You

When hateful thoughts hold you - neck, arms, legs
twisted into their lock, when they wrestle you down,
when your struggle against them serves only to tighten their
grip, and whatever has happened outside, this is inside

your own skin, these are your own, then you can call out
to water and wave, to darkness and light, to sand underfoot,
branching tree, moving breeze, to the music of crickets, the
stillness of stone, the distance of stars, you can call out

to a thousand gentle hands ready to lift, to soothe and to stroke,
comfort, console, hands your flesh knows, their ancient touch
sure, old ones who have always loved you. You can call out

to these most venerable midwives, feel their wrinkled hands ready
to catch your soft head, but groaning and writhing, it's you,
when the time is ripe, you, they'll require to push yourself out.

## Could It Have Been the Fine Thread?

*What have you ever traveled toward more than your own safety?*
                                                            –Lucille Clifton

Could it have been the fine thread, the shimmer connecting
the moon and your body, the way you both have of knowing
the rabbit must sometime jump back into the magician's
deep hat, that the art of vanishing also is magic, so that once

every month you shrugged off the whole innermost skin of yourself,
your future, all that you might have become if only the right seed
had come shooting in through your door, but it didn't, so you let it go,
disappear, like the round of the moon, white rabbit leaping

into the night's darkened hat, and if you had followed it there,
lost child wrapped in its blanket of blood, to the place where
all the dreams go, if you had taken that full shining face

between your own hands, looked into those eyes so eager to exist,
wouldn't you have felt the tug of that thread, of whatever
you travel toward more than your own safety?

## The Childless Tech Writer Talks to Aphrodite

*We live/ in place of the many who stir only/ if we listen --William Stafford*
(1982)

I walk through January rain from my office–
where I compose procedures to calibrate controls–
to the Ladies' Room where I check the blood rain
between my thighs.

My seasons have changed.
The arid months are past,
their bright summer showers
lasted only two days every month.
Now I make dark pools, pour down blood
for a full week. I'm halfway
to the age when rain will stop.

Hundreds of lost eggs, full moons
from twenty years of menstrual tides–
I contemplate them like stars
shining in the night of possibilities refused.

I listen: they cry out for birth.
Every month was an abortion. I knew this.
Every possible child wanted to exist.

Sweet Aphrodite, count their lost voices,
recalibrate the control of my life.
Send me pleasures enough, tender goddess,
to assuage their appetites.

## Grandmother with Shawl
### (1999)

She has been carved
into green, umber, brown
swirls of color within marbled stone,
by a 38-year-old Zimbabwean carver
dying of AIDS.
 "Grandmother" he calls her.
"Grandmother with shawl."

Her small secret smile, her forehead
with furrows of worry or wonder
or time, the smooth shine
on her face as she inclines down,
as her whole being leans
into the long shawl
that she holds to her cheek.

Carved of the same stone
that she is, the shawl
doesn't know
if its role
is to comfort
or to be
comforted.

## The Lagoon at Cascade Lake
### (2000)

The lagoon, as she enters,
licks her all over
with its tongue
of welcoming laughter.

As her arms reach out
to pull her through the lagoon,
her heart opens and opens
and stretches so wide
that everything slides inside.

The ring of cedars and firs
cast their reflections.

The eagle soars
through the vast blue.

Green lily pads
with yellow lilies
float.

Light darts off the crisp
transparency of dragonfly wings,
and the iridescent blue bodies flash.

She swims through galaxies
of reflected sunlight
too bright to look in the eye.

As her arms reach out
to pull her through the lagoon,
her heart opens and opens
and stretches so wide
that everything
slides inside.

As she leaves the lagoon
she slips and crawls slowly, too

soon, up the half-submerged
smoothness of slate.

Her heart contracts
to a muscle that pounds
in her chest as she
grapples against gravity
to stand on dry land alone.

**Plucking Figs**
(1992)

Lifting fig leaves, I finger the dark
softness of these once upright little
green fruits now swollen to drooping
purple. Thrill of the forbidden: as if
I am a child touching the soft
sacklets hung from my papa's puzzling
body, or a girl of nineteen grasping
the same sacks on the bucking body
of a lover, squeezing until they almost
seem to burst, shooting seeds of bright
light through my body. Biting through
the dark skin, my teeth sink into sweet
pink and white, sweet flesh configured
like an army of tadpoles plunging toward
shore. Maybe they'll keep on swimming
inside me, get kissed, grow into kings.

## Her Body
   (1999)

Her body is a fucking
fundamentalist—
monotheistic, monogamous, devout.
Her body holds the body of her beloved
as her Bible,
admits no other sources of revelation,
surrenders herself to the absolute truth
of her pleasure.

Her intellect is a secular humanist.
It reminds her that she must follow
more than one sacred text
through the world.
Not one of them can she neglect.
Her intellect expects her to close her legs
as easily as she would close a book.

**Red and Purple Verbena**
   (1999)

The tiger swallowtail's wings,
translucent and pale yellow parchment traced
with black strokes of calligrapher's ink,
seem to encode a lost music,
a silent swallowtail sonata
she can't quite hear or read,
a silent swallowtail sonata
that flutters in the summer sun
among hanging pots of red and purple verbena,
a silent swallowtail sonata
that brushes her cheek with its wing.

Though it settles on the purple verbena,
the swallowtail arrived only after they'd planted the red.
As she sits in the silence of this swallowtail sonata,
She thinks of her lover's hands pressing into the soil
between cedar pot's edge and wide-spread roots
of purple verbena. While her lover worked so
gently to make room for the red, she thought
of those same fingers opening and entering her,
pressing in deeper and deeper with all
of their need, giving way to those great pelvic thrusts
that shake the ground of her being, how her lover plunges
into her center again and again and again, into the place
where her soul hides, crouching in terror,
terror her lover's touch transmutes into ripples of light.

Though the swallowtail arrived when they planted the red,
it settles down now on the purple.
As she sits in the silence of this swallowtail sonata,
she thinks of her partner, who watched hummingbirds sip
from another purple verbena, for whose sake
she bought these, and found the recycled give-away cedar pots.
Her partner, who has taught her slowly that love and loyalty
are possible in this world, that the life of the kitchen
can be peaceful, and pulse with the pleasure of days.
She thinks of how, when she'd break a glass or a plate or a vase,
her partner would smile and say "It 's only a glass," or a plate, or a vase,

the sparkle in her partner's eyes making clear "You who broke it
are much more precious than this," until her runaway
heart could slow down to the pace of their quiet, shared days.

When the hummingbirds didn't come,
she bought red verbena, asked her lover
to transplant it during her stay.
Swallowtails came, no hummingbirds yet,
just butterflies so close and so present
she can almost read
the illuminated text of their wings.

Now red and purple verbena bask
in the interplay of their colors,
each made more brilliant by contrast
with the other. Each seems at peace
and at home within the shared pot.
Beneath the surface
their roots are weaving themselves together,
working out how to grow in such a tight space,
while in air, tiger butterflies flutter
their musically inscripted wings,
and the silence of the swallowtail sonata
seems to hover above the verbena
blessing both purple and red.

## Annunciation
### (1999)

In his monastery in Florence
Fra Angelico paints Gabriel
in a peach gown with rainbow wings
the colors of sunrise: wine, gray, peach, gold.

Gabriel, genuflecting as the sky does
every morning at dawn to the earth,
greets Mary, and he seems
to be singing his greeting,
as the sun also might seem to be singing at dawn,
perhaps Schubert's Ave Maria, music
that would make even an archangel weep.

The annunciation is real, it really does
take place morning after morning,
just as Fra Angelico paints it,
here under the arches of his own
medieval monastery in Florence.

In his painting, Mary's cloak is dark blue,
it is being cast off, she is emerging
from the cocoon of night
into the day-lit gold of her gown,
just as the rotating earth
steps forth every dawn into sun.

The annunciation really does take place
in biblical times, just as it takes place now,
story opening into its own eternity,
colorful wings spreading each day,
angel of heaven down on his knee
tenderly announcing to virgin earth
as if she has never been through this before
how she will give birth to this day–
child of God, savior of the world–
how beautiful it will be, and how sad.

# The Song of the Stars

## In the Dark of Your Mind
### (1978)

No one can find the way for you.
The only lights are the fireflies
and they don't even know you:
they play their own mating game.
When two join, their lights combine,
for a moment grow steady,
and, if you're quick,
you get a glimpse of the scenery.

So also when certain words join.

## I Speak
(1966)

Images you want, and wait for,
feelings inarticulate, or
reason's solemn caricature.

No, I have not brought it.
Ask a perfect question
if you seek reply.
Perfects punctuate themselves,
self-encircling arguments,
subjects are their objects.

What transitivity you wish,
supply. I shall not.
I am no mirror. I am not
a postulate.

I am stray ones, words,
arrived at your door.
You may open
but must issue
no invitation.

I am not suppliant or
accidental.
Carolling I come
bringing lyric answering
to all unaskeds.

**On Leaving My Job To Become a "Serious" Poet**
(1992)

None of us knows, what it means to step over the cliff,
clutching no more than a poetry book, a thin thread
leading back to a few fragile dreams,
subtle, elusive, as easily blown about as the fluff
of a dandelion, silken white feathers that ride on the wind
and discover for themselves that they are living seeds,
able to take root in the human heart,
until poems grow everywhere like weeds.

## Waiting
### (2001)

So, it's painful to wait and have nobody come.
Sitting on the steps after school, after
all the other kids have gone home,
waiting for your mother, knowing
she just might forget you, the way
she's always forgetting the keys,
her purse, her glasses, even the airplane tickets
for you to fly home to your father.

That's the courage your muse asks.
Another poet's muse might come daily and freely
tossing poems and poems and poems up into the air,
more than they ever could catch. But this
sitting alone on the concrete steps
of Bishop McGuinness High School
waiting for your own improbable mother who,
even though you know she might never come,
you would not trade now for anyone else's mother,
this muse is yours.

## Prayer to My Muse
### (1992)

Sometimes you come as a slender man
who, in spite of feminism, opens doors,
helps me to find my lost shoes, purse, car,
wants to feed me, to watch me enjoy
the world's most exquisite food,
whom I can bring with me even into the sacred spring
where Artemis and her nymphs still play, naked and whole,
who is blessed with such reverence that even the
virgin goddess gazes on him without rancor or rage.

Sometimes you are my dog faithfully waiting outside,
growling softly to let me know you are there, though I
am not aware of your presence until by chance I open the door.

Sometimes you are Neruda, with tongue and fingers
of green, with heart so open to life and poetry
that just to be near you is to place my finger into a socket of love
and be flooded by current beyond what my nerves can bear,
yet despite the shock of your presence, your absence is
far more terrible, in which I become leaf without wind,
wave without water, mouth without tongue,
song without voice, heart without blood.

## The Poet as Narcissus
### (1978)

If you were flesh, if you could touch the ground,
if I could know you, sinew, skin and bone,
touch your tentative fingers, smell your own
reclusive curls, spread my ear around
your soft-petaled sighs, dive in and swim
your surging sea, taste your frolicking
tongue, take in all the churning
love your lashing body could loose in
mine, if I could suck sink sigh rise crystallize
cling contract and explode in our shared cries,
then loose my limbs to ease you deeper in,
if I could clasp you in full silence, twin,
        would I sit here alone by this abyss,
        and wait for words to simulate our kiss?

**The Song of the Stars**
   (2001)

The stars in their
language of light
cradle each tiny
speck of stardust.

Could we but
understand
their song might
for all the pain
in the world
forgive and
console us.

## My Bright-Eyed Baby
(1965)

My bright-eyed baby is the night
so softly does she babble
her sparkling secrets
she imparts
in infantile chatter.

There was a world
before I came
without a night.
My bright-eyed baby is the night
murmuring my name.

My bright-eyed baby is the night
though I shall never scold her.
My bright-eyed baby is the night
and I alone may hold her.

## Spider Song
### (1973)

I am the artist here.
This easel is mine.
This silk thread, this self-thread, unwinds,
it is paint.
I hold the pointed brush poised,
I know the exact moment, I stroke
in utter perfection upon
fragile, remarkable space.

This may be my karma,
it may be the code in my genes.
Nevertheless, it is deliberate.
The spokes grow from a single center
tying together a scatter of branches,
and the circles—
the circles are magical—
a set of caught ripples.

Clear space is my canvas.
Clear space that is hung
among wider dimensions.
How delicately it is suspended there,
a bare glass window.
How transparent it is,
of an imperceptible thinness.

This fragility haunts me.
It wants me to protect it.
I want it intact
and to see through it clearly.
But there is a danger in seeing clearly,
a definite danger in unscratched glass
exposing itself too openly,
an invitation to breakage.

It is for this
that I scar our window
mimicking cracks. My web

is a delicate veil
spread over the glass.
What a web of illusions it is,
what a mask.
A fine lace curtain
trying to camouflage glass.
Not camouflage, but a child's disguise.
Will danger be touched, and not smash?

## Mescalina
(1978)

In a way I've always understood the language
that earth spells out against my mind.
I've known what she's been trying to tell me,
her long memory,
the billion years she's trying to explain.

But Mescalina, Mescalina,
devil-woman with the dangerous eye,
you lift the scales from my senses,
you melt the calluses from my mind.
Mescalina, Mescalina,
you make the world new and strange.

The breeze knows the melody she makes now,
the leaves know the reason that they dance.
My heart knows all about the rhythm that she keeps,
we each know exactly where we're going.
It's a great parade to a stirring music,
we're marching with a single longing,
that seems to twirl and fly
right before my eye,
it's the bright baton
of Mescalina.

But Mescalina, Mescalina
devil-woman with the dangerous eye,
you mock me with the longing and the music,
you mock me by lifting off the scales and calluses,
but I do love you, Mescalina,
though you laugh as you leave me behind.

The rapture becomes a dying echo.
I take up the slow work with the language and feel grateful,
with this net that seems too coarse to comprehend a whale,
to cast for the darting minnows of my mind.
If I catch them I only set them free again,
but the slow practice of casting I keep,
solid company for a long journey.

**Ruffian**
    (1976)

> *No horse ever outran her. Because she was a filly, she raced against fillies. The day they raced her against a colt, she broke her leg running. She couldn't stop, she kept coming down on the ankle stump, her hoof bent forward. They tried to repair her leg. After the long anesthetic sleep of surgery, she woke in a small stall, men holding her down, a heavy steel and plaster cast on her leg. She threw off the men and the cast. She threw herself against the walls. She was given a shot of phenobarbital, and she died.*

1.
It's true you were
bigger and stronger than most of the colts
famous filly
but why
did you try so hard?
For what
did you break your leg and
die at three years old?

For the three hundred thousand dollars
provided by network TV?
For the eight million viewers?

Even now, buried at Belmont,
your bones need years of rest
after the pounding you gave them.

Didn't you know they were only borrowed?
Didn't you know how delicate they were?

2,
Ruffian, here's what I'm dreaming.
You're a survivor
reaching for old age slowly
like a tree.
Slowly growing
gradually knowing

146

what the shape of your life will be.

It is not mostly racing
though that rare
wild flute fire does still blow through.
Mostly
you live quietly here
where one careful footstep
follows another.

And your legs, your bones.
You care for those
like porcelain
more fired than fire
more transfigured than wind.

3.
I am the flute flying into the wind.

4.
I am the fire rising out of the bird.

5.
I am the flotsam the whirlwind whirls.

6.
Do you see the stable boy holding my head in his arms?
I am the slow tear traversing the miles from my eye to his hand.
He knows he can't save me. The others think that they can.

7.
A dark horse comes from behind
trying to pass.
I have never run so fast.
Men hold me back,
I shake them off, small flies,
this is my big match.
All of my life has been practice for this.

8.
From fine white clay

the mother potter made you
on her whirling world wheel
bone by bone.

Now you return her perfect porcelain pieces.

Her stock of clay is small.
She must reuse it all.

9.
Ruffian lies buried in mystery
where tragedy transmutes to triumph and back again
where white bones stand out against the rich brown soil
her flesh is crumbling to, bones like hieroglyphs,
stark lines and curves, secret messengers
of the mystery of running
sent down in runes to another reality.

10.
My words are her bones.

## Mary at Six, Watering Grass
(1976)

Her mind is empty of thoughts,
her toes between leaves of grass,
    fearless of words,
      forget the past.
Her hands do not grasp
at the sun's slow pass.

Her future is free from dread
but the stir of Christmas, promises,
raises her pulse to a hummingbird pitch.

The cat's dead body decomposes
under the honeysuckle bush.
Blossoms bleed honey fragrance
while hidden roots suck sustenance
from vanishing bones.
She does not mourn.

She aims her hose high,
the arching stream,
silver in sunlight,
begins to sing.

## The Big Dipper
    (2000)

I wish that I could offer its lips to your lips,
       that I could hold it by its handle of stars
       and dip it into the abyss of the universe,
and let you sip from it,
       that I could fill it with the mystery and
       music of our very existence,
and let you sip from it,
and slowly drink,
       let you drink so deeply from it,
that you would never again
       feel thirst.

## Looking for the Words
### (1978)

I'm looking for the words
I want to write
with my whole heart.

I'm looking for the words
that are rightfully mine.

I'm looking for the words
that will fit inside this moment,
the way petals fit inside a rose.

***

I'm looking for the voice
that is really my own.

I'm looking for the voice
that my tongue could use
to whisper in my own ear.

I'm looking for the voice
of love and recognition
but it's such a foggy morning
that I can't hardly hear.

***

I got this great big hole inside
and it's sucking all my life away.
It's like a vacuum cleaner, won't let anything stay.
It eats all the words I find it
and there's nothing left for me.

Well I know that words with rhythm
if they're made of real clear pictures
can escape the vacuum cleaner
but the trouble is they don't mean much to me.

All my poems that make pictures
are as cold as little trophies
I want words that'll cuddle with me.

***

I got a door between the parts of me.
If it opens then I'm gonna be free,
with a universe of stars spilling out into my skies,
and as many eyes open in me.

***

I gotta get through this old hole inside
it's an old exploded memory
I was raped as a young child
and it vanished from my mind
leaving nothing but this gaping hole behind.

Well, I've been there one time
and I'm not going back no more.
Yeah, I've been there one time
and I'm not going back no more.

But I think that hole,
it might just be the door.
Yeah, I think that hole,
it might just be the door.

***

I know somewhere deep inside
are the words I'm looking for.
There's a voice already singing,
way beyond the fog.
It's a spring rising up in me,
it's an innocent, original melody,
and it's clear water, that's all,
rising out of where the hole used to be.

## Drinking the Dark
### (1976)

 My soul, you stand by your well.
The coolest blue water in the world
looks black to you.
The thirstiest woman in the world
asks you for a drink.
You think your water too dark for her.

All night you look down
into the black well bottom.
Our Lady of Dark Skies
opens her peacock throat
a mandala of eyes.
The black looks back at you.

You offer the woman a drink.
You apologize
for dark water, you speak
of stars and eyes and distances, you speak
silk threads weaving a sweet cocoon.
You speak to a woman becoming the moon.
You have filled her again.

## For Simone Weil
### (1976)

This is no curtain, my love, this last black place.
It is the face
of the everlasting,
the void.
It is God's empty face and his million glittering stars.

Do you feel your size,
my soul,
how small you are in this measureless night?

Look into the black uncertainties now
and count
how many eyes search the same abyss
from how many worlds.

Your birth and death
mean nothing to them, those faraway eyes,
the death of your sun,
a tiny flickering in their skies.

You silence your heart to overhear their thoughts.
Wind rustles the banana leaves.
A chorus of crickets
sings.

All week you have wondered why
the crickets sing,
whether they answer each other.

Now you know
they sing to the numberless strangers
that live in the stars,
they launch their song in the void,
their brief perfume
wings its way home.

You are Noah, you ride
on this world, your arc,
through a flood of dark and distances.

You send out your song,
a dove.

## Before You Make a Poem
(1993)

Know that only part of the poem comes from you.
Part comes from beyond, from the little girl
with slow tremulous feet who thrusts
her four-legged walker so it leaps
in front of her like a horse, infused
with a spirit her body can't fully incarnate;
or from the great heron that rises
above a pond, impressing on the moment
the silver-blue spread of its wings.

And you're pierced with another world.
A new thing wants to be born. So you take
the words, and you build it a house, you shape it
a body. If you're lucky, it lives. Or it's stillborn,
body without breath, uninhabited house.
The breath flutters off, great blue heron
fleeing the intruding presence in its pond,
or the body, born with faltering muscles
beyond your control, stumbles and falls.
Whether it lives or dies, breathes,
stumbles or soars, the poem is never yours.

Nor can you, left behind, compare your work
with others. Their poems may breathe and soar,
but the same bits of the universe don't knock
at their door, don't ask for their help being born.
What calls on you can call only on you.
You might as well trust yourself then.
Hold the poem like the egg of a wild bird
in the warmth of your hand. In the moment
of making, its blue wings touch the edges
of everything.

## On The Threshold of a Poem
### (1997)

This stone threshold is rubbed smooth
from long use.
It is old.
Your feet can step through it bare.
But beware.
On the other side,
temples have crumbled with time,
museums have been shattered by war,
their rubble and shards are everywhere.

Only this fragile gateway remains intact
and the butterfly whose
red and black wings
fluttering like a tongue
instruct you
in the accidental
unspeakable
silence
you can't bear alone.

**If I go away...**
      for MSM
      (2004)

"If I go away
before you die,
will you write me
a poem?"
Your eyes fill
with tears
as I hear
my voice
saying yes
and I think of
the distance
between us
the silence
between
all human being
the distance
I've ceased
to rail against
with poem
after poem
after poem
how I've rested
years
in the silence
of not
writing poems,
no poems
for years
to claw and tear
at my heart,
no poems
ceaselessly
striving to speak
what cannot
be spoken.
Your question
rousing me now

from this good rest:
now the sound
of my voice
saying
yes

**Pulsating Poem**
(2002)

*In 1915, Einstein's general theory of relativity changed forever our view of the universe. One of the theory's signal legacies is the idea that the seemingly distinct properties of three-dimensional space and one-dimensional time are actually woven together into a seamless, four-dimensional "spacetime," with a "fabric" that can be distorted, curved, and warped by the gravity of large objects... such as "frame dragging" -- the wrinkling and pulling of the fabric of spacetime in the presence of massive, rapidly spinning objects such as neutron stars.*

*...Steinhardt and Turok... offered an intriguing new twist on an old alternative to the conventional big-bang theory: a "pulsating" model that posits an endless cycle of big bangs that give rise to our visible, 4-D universe -- followed, after trillions of years, by "big crunches" that set the stage for the next expansion. What sets the new model apart is that it takes its lead from string theory, and in particular from the string-theoretic notion that we live in a vast, sheetlike 4-D membrane, or "brane," embedded within a higher-dimensional spacetime. In the new model, the repeated collision and separation of two such infinite branes -- ours, and a "mirror universe" only a fraction of a meter away -- give rise to the universe's endlessly repeating bang-and-crunch life cycle ... the cyclic model actually harmonizes well with some recent observations that are hard to square with classic big-bang theory*–from May 2002 Science Roundup (American Association for the Advancement of Science member services newsletter summarizing articles in Science magazine)

String theory,
eyes bleary,
neutron star
pulls us far
out of linearity -
get the similarity?
Twist and pull,
bang and crunch,
the pulsating
universe,
bang explo-
sion, crunch implo-
sion with its mir-
ror universe
It's self mating –

(could be worse).
Gravity,
Relativity,
massive rapid
spinning objects
wrinkle all
eternity,
pull  on
every
galaxy,
even pull on
you and me.
Just beyond
big bang
horizon,
cosmic scale
"get outa jail,"
quantum-scale
probabil-
ity bail,
human scale
succeed or fail–
snake that swallows
its own tail.
Catch that space-time
ball and run,
play the field and
have some fun,
black holes are
for everyone,
shake that space-time
4-D sheet,
shake it bake it
make it sweet.
Meet that mir-
ror universe,
craft that crunch
into a kiss,
clang that bang
into sheer bliss,
spin now spin,

pull cosmic strings,
spin from every
golden fleece,
be both spinner
and the wheel,
be both violin
and player,
you can't know
on just what scale
chance and choice
succeed and fail
harmony
disharmony
war and peace
cosmic reach
quantum peach
neutron stars
candy bars
public herds
poets' words
distort warp
crease and curve
any given
situation,
twist the fabric
of a nation,
into your unique
creation.
Giving up is
the temptation,
dropping out of
the pulsation.
Cosmic scale
numerate
at the cosmic
scale gate
many many
powers of ten
numerate
again and again,
quantum scale

denominate
at the quantum
scale gate
many minus
powers of ten
denominate
again
and again,
human scale
succeed or fail -
snake that swallows
its own tail.
Count the fingers
on your hand,
digitate and
calculate,
calculate the
power of ten,
moving power
of one life
moving power
of one hour,
power of
one is
power of ten —
(better figure
that again).
Crunch and bang,
kiss and run,
hold the rhythm,
have some fun,
cast the spell,
be a center
of creation,
be a center
of the nation,
clapping hands,
slapping hands,
now slip up and
down the scale,
multiply,

and now divide,
numerate,
denominate,
powers of ten
by powers of ten,
moving hands
two foreign lands
mir-roar self
and universe,
both pulsating
both gyrating
both creating
both debating
inundating
fabricating
annotating
biodegrading
masquerading
lamentating
boxing crating
mincing grating
menstruating
loving hating
masturbating
there's no ending
there's no start
just pulsating
just pulsate
throb and beat
thud and pulse
thump and pound
bang and crunch
bang and crunch
bang and crunch -
The universe
is out to lunch.
String theory,
eyes bleary,
neutron star
pulls us far
out of linearity -

get the similarity?
Twist and pull
bang and crunch
the pulsating
universe,
it's self mating –
(could be worse).
Gravity,
Relativity,
massive rapid
spinning objects
wrinkle all
eternity,
pull  on
every galaxy,
even pull on
you and me.
Just beyond
big bang horizon,
cosmic scale
"get out of jail,"
quantum-scale
probabil-
ity bail,
human scale
succeed or fail -
snake that swallows
its own tail.
Catch that spacetime
ball and run,
play the field and
have some fun,
black holes are
for everyone,
shake that spacetime
4D sheet,
shake it bake it
make it sweet.
Meet the mirror
universe,
craft the crunch

into a kiss
clang the bang
into a bell
turn in side out -
HEAVEN
from hell!

# Sorrows of Departure

Poems Written For Drawings by Romaine Brooks
(1978-1980)

In the 1970s, gay liberation and the women's movement made it possible
for me to embrace my lesbian identity in a way that would not have been
possible if I had lived in an earlier generation. This gift came with a price
similar to that exacted of the immigrant who is given a whole new world
of opportunities and freedom in exchange for giving up the continuity and
connections of the old. This loss of continuity led to a search for historical
lesbians whom I could embrace as foremothers, and look to as models, and
from whom I could develop a sense of rootedness in the larger human story.

When I read Diane Middlebrooks' biography of the artist Romaine Brooks I
was very drawn to the drawings Middlebrooks used as chapter heads. Later I
found Adelyn Breskin's book, *Romaine Brooks. Thief of Souls* and discovered
more of Brooks' drawings.

These drawings spoke so intimately to my own inner life (as they still do) that
the process of contemplating them and composing companion poems had a
quality similar to communion with an ancestral spirit.

I am grateful to Richard Sorenson and Leslie Green of the Smithsonian
Institute American Art Museum for permission to reproduce the drawings.
I am grateful to Romaine Brooks for creating them, and for the fact that,
across differences of class and epoch and experience, they gave me human
connection and knowledge that I was not alone in this world.

Note: The titles of the poems are the titles Brooks gave to the drawings.

## ANGELS FEED THE SAINT'S DONKEY

The saint sleeps in the quiet pool of her being,
close to the earth, hand a curved crescent moon,
head cradled in elbow,
the saint's dog, soft cheek against foreleg,
cuddled in the same still sleep.

A halo the shape of an egg hovers above her
and angels rise out of her sleep.
Visions stream between angels' eyes.
Their hands reach out, they offer
"here, do you want to eat?"
The donkey, humble creature who has
born the savior to Bethlehem,
ears slightly back, wary of visitation,
the donkey eats from the hand of an angel.

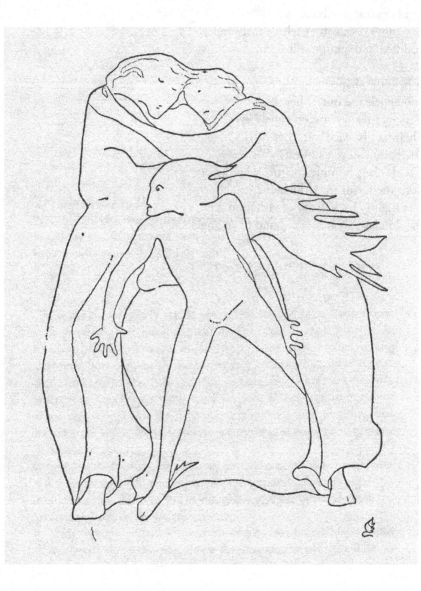

## TIME SEPARATES

Two women lean into each other.
Their mature years consolidate to a mountain
of comfort. Heads angle together, rest,
arms melt around shoulders,
hair taking root in each other's heads.
Out from under the cloak of their union,
Time springs, a child who was hiding there,
frightened. Time's hair bursts into fire,
she parts the women like curtains,
looks quickly around
and runs.

## CAUGHT (also IMPRISONED or IN PRISON)

One demon is languid, arm
a limp curve, snout drooping.
The woman's foot climbs to the demon's shoulder
as if to step from him to heaven.
A second demon crouches on the woman's knee,
his back arched, his hand gripping her shoulder.
His head flames into the head of demon three,
who grabs her from behind,
claws into her ribs, curls his toes
over the edge of a cliff.
In the midst of demons, imprisoned and pulled,
she reaches out, catches one by the shoulder,
and ascends the ladder of her tormenters.

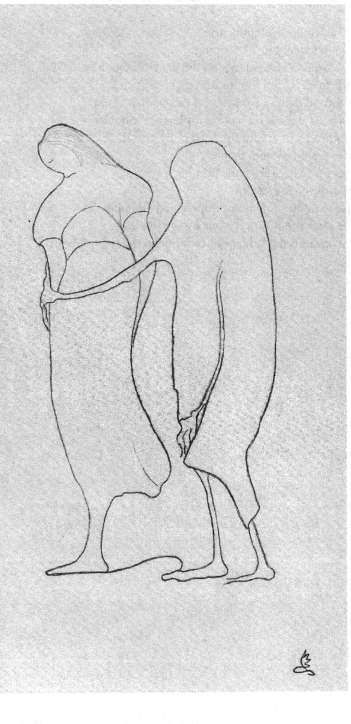

## DEATH AND THE PEASANT

Death is featureless, nearly formless,
a shy creature that stands just behind,
his frail arm intervenes between her
and the world. She is taller than death,
well-formed, large-armed, but she yields.
Her foot that has been firm on the earth
extends on the curve of a line that leads
to death's foot.
Maybe death needs her
to strengthen his incomplete being.
Maybe she gives herself to him.
Maybe death is protecting her from the world.

# EQUILIBRIUM – DEATH'S TOY

The balancer wears loose clothes,
perhaps is a student of tai chi or aikido,
of forces that configure body and energy.
For her, to remain alive is an exercise
in immense concentration.
To survive, she surrenders her boundaries,
bleeds out through her hands into the world,
while her foot firmly planted becomes one
with the shifting surface on which she balances.
Underneath the surface, death stoops.
He nods and shrugs, tilting the universe,
until the balancer falls.

## FOOT-STOOL

The model is motionless, legs tucked underneath,
weight tilted back, propped on one arm,
as she was positioned. Round breasts,
round belly, empty eyes round
as after shock. The artist has thin hips,
he steps from her shoulder onto her head.
She is the foot-stool on which he approaches his god,
the rock he wishes he were chiseled from.
He becomes his destination. She allows
her life fluids to leak through her hand.
By spilling herself, she imagines she can
float, on her own being, home.

## HEADDRESS

The woman's head is imprisoned in a stocking.
Tightly woven fabric stretches across her features,
comes between her lips and the breathing world.
Her head bows to her fate, but her hair
pushes through, stubborn grass growing toward light.

## THE IMPEDERS

Tucked under the wing of an angel-horse, the woman rises
toward her own angelic being.  One impeder squats,
seizes the tail over his head, leans with his full weight, and
pulls. The other impeder bends his knees deep, curves his back
into a taut bow, shoulders stretched, arms perfectly straight.
As the woman's foot lifts from the earth, the two angel faces
turn and look back. Their beatific gaze falls on the faces,
transfigured with fear, of the impeders. The angels will die
if they touch the earth: still, they comfort the impeders
with their eyes.

# THE IDIOT AND THE ANGEL

The idiot is a captive of gravity.
His head wobbles on a neck of rubber,
the corners of his eyes droop.
The shoulders slump, even the shapeless coat pulls
toward the ground. The legs are tremors, lack bones,
and the long limp arms, open at the wrist,
end in emptiness instead of hands.
Each step could be his last, the foot that bears
his weight loses itself to the ground.
The angel, her brother's keeper, spreads
her strong wing, resists the forces
that push him down.
She summons the slack mouth,
the wavering eyes. Her lips are firm,
her eyes focus with stern compassion
as she leads the idiot toward stairs.

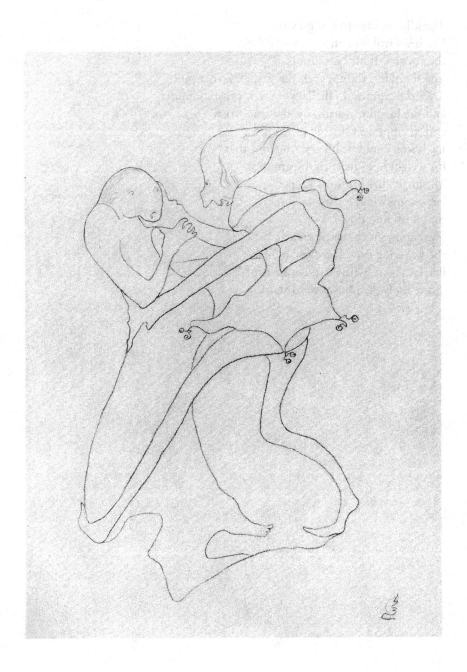

## THE JESTER AT HOME

Bursting out of his cute little bell-trimmed frock,
the jester seizes his pregnant wife,
jabs a large thumb into her timid cheek,
yanks at the weary small of her back.
She shrinks and tugs at his wrist,
as if to parry the attack, but
her dress suggests, in its languidness,
a welcome to the vigor of his step.
His legs, grown long and agile on her fear, advance.
He thrives on forcing her open:
peaceful acts of intercourse bore him.
To penetrate the tender lips of her fear,
to pound on the soft new skull of her future child,
relieves him. Rape sustains his sense of humor.

# LETHE

The woman is naked and without human company.
Tension melts out of her life, her cheek
rests on her own shoulder. Her eyes close
softly,  the eyes of a sleeping child.
She is draped, with an ease she
has never experienced before,
on rock formations that rise out of water.
They seem to be made for her,
these strange and living furnishings
of her final hour.
Great birds lean forward to follow,
with enormous solicitous eyes,
her foot as it eases itself into Lethe,
blossoming ripples of silence.
Even the rock, grown into the shape
of a contorted tree, has consciousness here,
its open eye strains to glimpse
the hand resting so delicately
on its forehead.
Lethe, the river, is tender
and washes away the woman's pain.

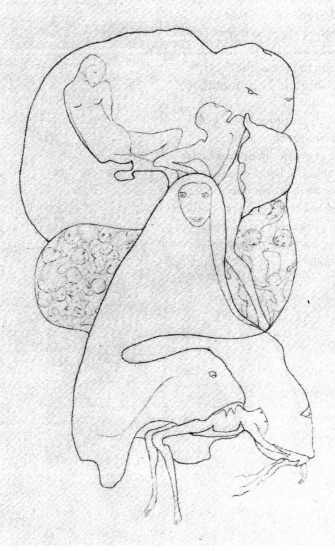

# MOTHER NATURE

Nature, the virgin mother, occupies center,
her face open, inexperienced.
Behind her, infants float in Nature, the womb
that incubates them into the dreamy
bodies of childhood, out of which
they are snatched by Nature in the form of a thief,
Nature with narrow shifty eyes, neck hunched
into shoulders, Nature who keeps them
until she grows bored, then lets them drop
into the jaws of Nature, the devouring eel.
Nature, who swallows their limp bodies whole,
their long legs and hair trailing briefly
out of her sharp-toothed mouth, until,
swirled back into her innocent belly,
Nature's children are again made new.

## THE MUMMY (also STOLEN MUMMY)

He is limber and huge
a vast naked genie out of Arabian Nights
who awakens, not from inside of a vase,
but from the mummy's own loosening tapes.
Unwinding, they eddy like live snakes,
have a will of their own. They conjure
his stronger existence, which
snatches her out of the tomb.
The tapes wind over his thigh and calf,
drape across his ankle, slide between his toes,
loop and tie around his elbow
and encircle the newborn surprise
on his face. She remains rigid,
resists the unwinding tapes,
furrows her forehead, glowers,
pulls her petulant mouth down,
but her obedient slave is bound.
He must act out the will she denies.

# THE ORGAN GRINDER

The organ protrudes, tumorous, from under
the paunch of the stubby-legged grinder.
Its one tapered leg searches the street, eager
as a Geiger counter or an anteater's snout.
Tied by a noose to the grinder's neck,
the organ leads him.
His spine reverberates music,
the tassel on his cap dances,
he follows the organ, grinding and grinding.
For years, his lips have worn a habitual pout
and his eyes have strained up, as he waits for God
to deliver him from too heavy a cross,
too demanding an instrument.

## THE PAST (also THE PAST – DEPART)

The traveler stops.
Her suitcase serves as a bench.
Her elbows lean on the wall,
and her eyes drift across waves
to a shore that only exists
in the mind of a woman
she can't be anymore.
The salt breeze of another world
tugs at her shawl.

## PRIMITIVE COQUETRY

She adopts the posture she considers refined,
rises up onto her stocky hind-legs,
presses her hind-paws in at the heel,
out at the toe, retracts her uncivilized claws.
She stands with the unmentionable
underside between hind-legs carefully concealed,
thrusts her ribcage awkwardly forward,
presses the thick wrists of her forelegs together,
allows her forepaws to delicately dangle.
Suppressing the reflex wags of her small, vestigial tail,
she stretches her neck to an uncomfortable
angle and length, tucks her chin in,
glances out of an eye forced open
unnaturally wide. She attempts a coy glance,
but her lips part to reveal
an unmistakably canine smile.

## ROYALTY

Her eye bulges, the eye of a bullfrog
that puffs out its chest.
From her flat broad nose, nostrils flare,
her wide lips are held firmly closed.
Below the snug unattractive crown,
a lock of hair, pulled down, covers
her forehead, crosses the bridge of her nose.
Her earlobe, pierced by a large ring,
protrudes slightly from behind carefully
coifed hair. A string of pearls graces
her shoulder and neck, below which
she does not exist. She has traded her body
for a crown.

## THE SOLDIER AT HOME

The soldier at home is an awkward bird,
his waistcoat bunched like a fine lady's bustle,
his neck elongated, his starched collar
resembling the neckpiece of a nun.
Striking an ostrich pose, he holds his infant son
in two stubby wings, unaccustomed to flight.
His tied hair pokes out from under his helmet
and, at his pantaloons, an old dog leans
a warm nose, waits for his master to rub.
The soldier stands watch, his eyebrow
ominously cocked. As domestic tranquility
softens his mouth, his body stiffens,
resists. The soldier at home is on guard.

## SUPPLICATION

The lover stands naked and strong,
embraces her own head.
Eyes closed, she lets her cheek rest on her arm.
The other arm curves around her beloved
who stands beside her, dress caught in the wind.
The outsider is a supplicant on her knees,
bare feet exposed from under her long robe,
she clings to the naked lover's powerful torso,
tugs at the arm poised at the beloved's waist.
The two lovers, standing, draw sustenance
from each other's stance.
The tall lines of their bodies accentuate one another.
Without noticing, they exclude the supplicant
from the conspiracy of their strength.

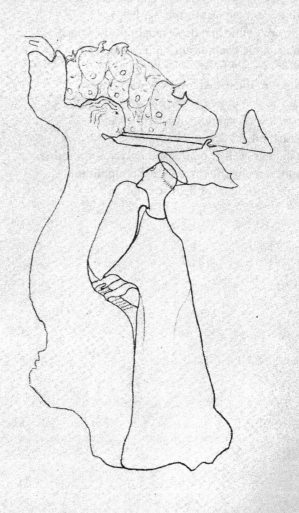

## WHAT THE SAINT HEARD AND SAW (also THE SAINT'S SURPRISE)

The hands of the saint are devout,
they humbly worship the piano.
Frail and monastic in the loose folds of his robe,
the saint raises his haloed head, his thin chin
points up toward the vision. The soul of the piano
has risen, one ghostly hand glides across air,
one hand supports a heavenly horn.
The saint's trembling fingers hardly dare
touch the familiar keyboard, as the piano's smooth
smiling lips kiss the lips of her horn.
The sound is a chorus of children,
eyelids closed in concentration,
mouths flung open in song.

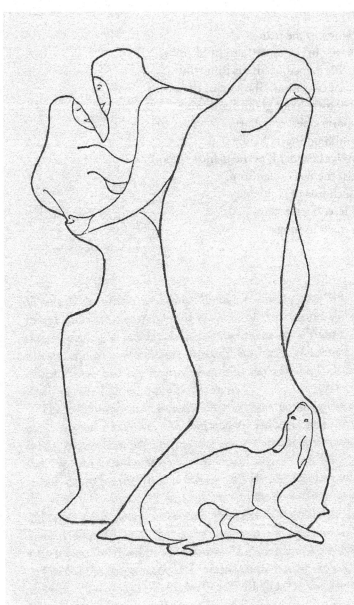

## WE WEEP AND WE WEEP ALONE

Behind the weeper, a lover leans
scooping another into her life. The other
bends to receive. Though she stands,
the receiver's back is supine, her weight
rests in her lover's arms. The lovers
draw close to each other, a bright gaze
binds their eyes, warm breaths
join their soft smiling lips.
The weeper stands apart, hides grief
in the folds of her robe, ignores
the loyal dog who comes close, creeping
along the boundary of her sorrow.

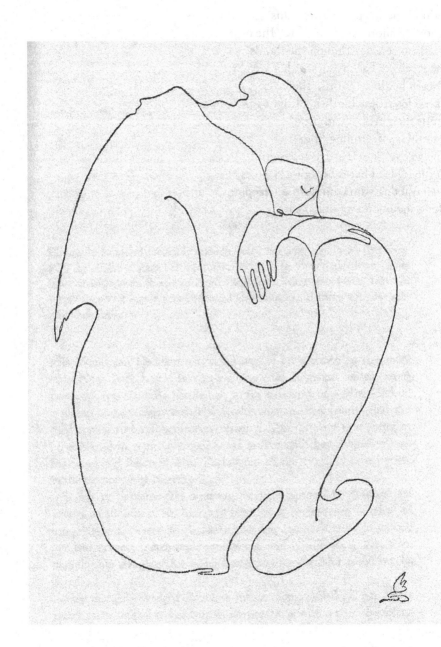

# DEPARTURE

Curled up like a sea creature
in a conch shell, departure comforts herself.
listens to her own heartbeat, her breath.
The curve of her arm flows
into the curve of her leg, the curl
of her foot. One hand rests on her own knee
as gently as a mother's hand rests on the head
of a child. The other hand nestles
inside the crook of her elbow.
Her head droops down toward the still place
in which, wrapped in herself,
departure rests.

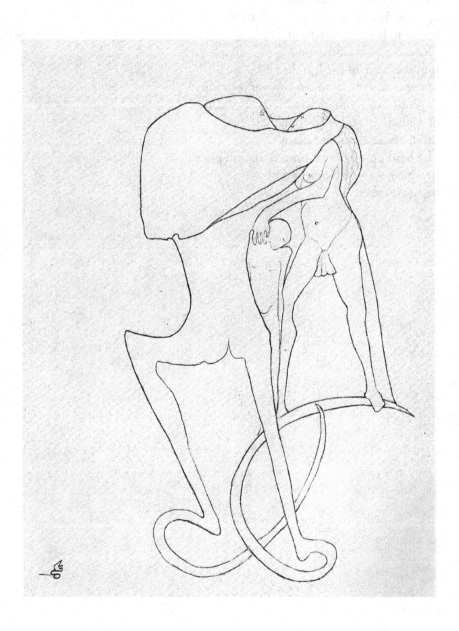

## TOMORROW RECLAIMS YESTERDAY AND TODAY

Tomorrow reclaims Yesterday:
his nonhuman face, with no features but eyes,
approaches Yesterday's face.
A hood or a cape hides half of Tomorrow's face.
He is armless, his cape lassoes Yesterday's head.
A grown woman, young, thick hair to her waist, breasts bare,
Yesterday wears only a soft cloth over her vulva.
Her hand shields a thin quivering child, Today,
who presses against her leg. Yesterday does not willingly yield.
She stands wide and strong, in the full power of pelvis and hips;
still, she cannot resist. The ground that she stands on
is his, is the long sickle foot of Tomorrow
on which, lurching and tripping, he claims
her and her child as his.

## ENEMY FAT

Enemy fat is immense, she comes
with great flapping breasts,
mountainous thighs, heavy arms, and
she pushes thick legs, pigeon-toed,
between the woman's own slender legs.
A fat thigh presses against the slim woman's
pubis, fat hands clasp her firm back, pull her
close to fat belly, fat breasts.
The woman claws at fat bulging cheeks,
fat ample arms. She appears to resist,
but does not summon her full strength to escape.
Instead, something thin in her sheds itself,
an old skin, leaves a nakedness open
to soft enveloping flesh,
longing for the enemy she dreads.

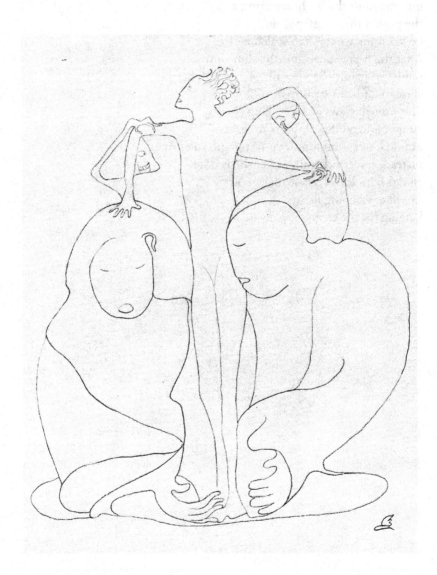

## THEIR CREATURES

The woman's hair sizzles, she searches
for deliverance. At her feet, low gentle beings
worship and give her shape. Eyes closed, they
listen to breath and sound, to the
messages of fingers, they scoop and round
their loose robes into her human feet.
The long fingers of one seem to strum
an invisible harp, the other's fingers are stubby
and strong, they pat on energy as palpable as stone.
At her elbows, skinny demons crudely create,
forcing her arms into odd, awkward shapes.
They pinch, measure, torment; their faces
stretch into great ogling grins.
Blind to their saboteurs, the low gentle beings
stay deep in devout meditation, ignore
all creatures they do not consciously create.

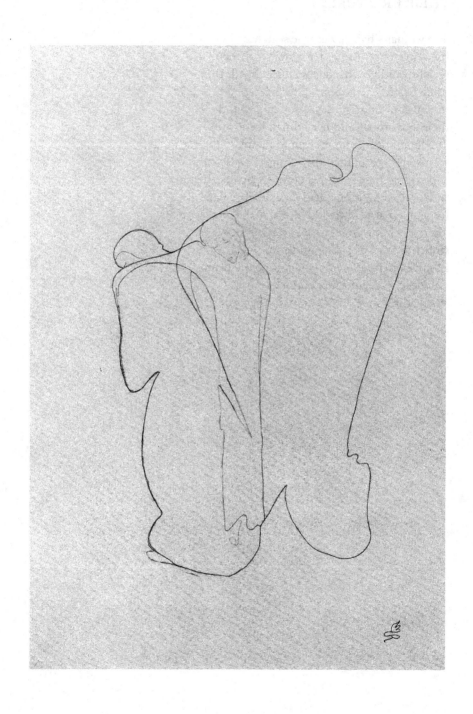

## SORROWS OF DEPARTURE

The traveler carries her history with her,
hunching forward to balance its weight.
On her back, a departing self lies in a coma,
its arm stretches across her shoulder,
its feverish face dangles loosely.
A wraith suspended between two worlds,
it does not exist in the world of flesh,
through which the solitary traveler trudges.
Nor does the departing self exist yet in history,
the conch shell on the traveler's back,
into which her lost selves slowly congeal.

When the traveler sleeps, she retreats
into her shell, touches the cool smooth
curves of memory, hears her spirit breathe
like the sea.

# No Goddess Dances to a Mortal Tune

Most of the poems in this section were published in chapbook form in 1992. They grew out of the vibrant first decade of my marriage to Chris Downing. Inspired by her lifelong passion for Greek mythology, these poems were in some sense composed as love poems to her.

Note: A passing acquaintance – preferably a friendship – with the stories of Greek mythology is essential to appreciating the poems in this section. If you're new to the stories, or need refreshing, Crowell's Handbook of Classical Mythology by Edward Tripp (Thomas Y. Crowell Co., NY, 1970) provides lively summaries, with references to classical sources for further reading. For a rich revisioning of the stories in relation to the psychology of women, see The Goddess: Mythological Images of the Feminine, by Christine Downing (iUniverse, NY, 2007).

The barest bones of the major stories referred to in these poems are available (based on Tripp) in my Mythological Notes at the back of this section, arranged in alphabetical order.

## Ode to Aphrodite
(1992)


Your ankle, Aphrodite, and the arch of your foot
as you step from the shell that has brought you ashore,
born as you are from the frolicking foam,
from the flash and glide of sun upon rolling waves,
Aphrodite, among all the gods, we know you best
through our flesh, perhaps because
of the way our clocks stop instantly
upon your arrival, as if from a power
failure or perhaps just a siphoning off
of electricity into our skins becoming cats,
caressing the very air that surrounds us and
purring with lust, our thighs pulsing and glowing
and growing as if into the huge and powerful
thighs of lion and lioness, while this strange precarious
preciousness, this rare gold, pounded to dust
and filling the air with its dazzling light,
this dangerous pleasure you bring,
blinds us to everything that does not shine as bright.

Sometimes you choose me as priestess–
forty-five, old enough to be unseen
by most men, but when you choose me
I know how each languid lift of my wrist,
flutter of eyelid, flicker of eye, how each
supine stretch of my smile, each undulation
of skirt, how the simple curve of my breast
ripples with your sparkling laughter, so that
a man, any man, no matter how usually smooth
with his tongue, will stumble and say
"I've heard so much about you, you are
practically a legend. It's great to meet you in
the          . Great, I mean, to meet you in the          ."

And a pause, as if he can't quite speak the word,
not in your presence, as if he does not dare to name
this usually frail stuff of which our human lives
are made, this stuff which in your presence

engorges with power, so that a woman's least little
finger, beckoning, is more compelling than guns.

## The Two Goddesses–and a God

### Persephone
   (1991)

At first it was only the lily
a kind of annunciation
as when Gabriel held it
singing birth birth birth
but that was another story.
         I bent to pick it, that lily,
and in that moment
was blessed: was at one
with the garland of girls
that danced in the meadow.
Softer than petals,
the blue up above,
the sun's bright caress.
Softer than petals,
the swirl of their skirts,
the brush of their maiden flesh.


                    And then the earth opened.
Seized by a tremor of darkness
and wrenched from the world I'd known,
darkness forced into my mouth
and between my teeth,
darkness thrust down my throat,
darkness thrust through my nose,
darkness thrust through my ears,
darkness forced into my eyes,
a fist of darkness between my thighs
tearing my insides,
                    and knowing
                    I was forever changed
                    forever different.
So it was Hades I wed,
King of Death,
God of the world below.

And where was my mother, oh goddess of all things that grow,
when his rough hands pulled me down to the root of it all?
Where was my mother and what was her power then,
when Hades took me like a calf or a dog or a bench
and made me a thing, a possession of his?
Where was my mother then, and where the dance of her golden grains?
        Do not
           talk to me about life and the living.
I am the wife of Hades,
I am His Queen.
The shades salute him, and I,
seated on the cold gold throne at his side,
I too am saluted.
Before me, as before him,
the Underworld bows.
At my every word now,
the Nether World cringes
and scurries to obey.
Even Cerberus the fierce
whines when I approach, and begs
for a pat from his mistress's hand.

As for me, I do not think
of my mother's soft eyes,
her bosom, her arms,
they are part of a life I have left,
torn from me by the dark.
Where was she
when the earth opened up
and swallowed my girlhood?

And now I am Queen.
I have grown somewhat fond of my power.
Do not think I partake innocently.
Do not think I mistake these pomegranate seeds.
I know they're the food of the dead:
seeds of power, seeds of blood.
I who was torn from the world of my mother
I know these seeds.
Before that moment, there was no force in my world,
life danced in my mother's sweet circles

of flowers and fruits, growing and grains,
but now things are different.
I'm frankly intrigued by the taste of command
and savor the ruby red seeds slowly
crushing them knowingly
between strong teeth no longer innocent.
It is Hades, my husband, who bids me cease,
knowing,
as those of my father's generation
do know,
that Destiny must be obeyed
even by gods.

And I go
as if I could be again the same girl I was,
soft skin  soft small bosom  soft eyes,
I, Queen of Death, Lady of Darkness,
I who rise from the earth
as the lily once did
as if to return to those innocent dances,
as if to rejoin that garland of girls,
as if my mother and I could be reunited,
as if the two goddesses could be made one.
She who blesses the earth with abundance,
she for whom flowers, grains, fruits grow once again,
she is my mother.
And I am her daughter, I,
in whom seeds of death are planted
and will sprout.

**Demeter**
(1991)

From the other side of the world child
I heard your scream
felt your abduction
in every pore of my skin
the stench of your violation,
the core of your sacred body defiled,
darkness forcing itself deep inside,
knowing I never prepared you for this.

Only the Sun would name the perpetrator,
but I should have known
who else could it be
but your father (his brother, what difference?):
male gods who long ago usurped
the power of our grandmothers,
those great ancient goddesses,
who being keepers of life
could not deny the gods their destiny.
I too, daughter, I am a keeper of life,
though while separate from you
I forget the world placed in my keeping.

And I mourn.
Nothing grows.
I reward small human kindnesses
and dream of giving immortality to a human child
as if somehow that would undo the harm
from which I could not preserve you.
But destiny, laughing, terrifies its mother
to intervene, and I a goddess
cannot do even this one small deed.
And I mourn.
Earth is barren, humans starve
baffled by this drama of the gods.

Daughter, do not imagine I deceive myself
or dream I can call you back as you were.
Nor do I dream of freeing you,
when you think of my absence, my failure,
from the hatred that hardens your eyes.
How can a goddess who makes the very grain to grow
allow her own child to be raped?

Do not be afraid: I know of your hate.
Even the goddesses, especially the goddesses
must dance with destiny, daughter.
Do not think I require you back as you were,
I know you are changed.
And I too, daughter, I also am changed,

227

oh flesh of my flesh,
these seeds of death within you,
they are seeds in my flesh.
I embrace all of you, daughter,
the change and the hate,
the longing to partake of your violator's power,
and I call you, I call you forth as you are
knowing you may not be able to love me now
in the face of my failed power,
power that seemed so great
to your child eyes.

You will never know Persephone
except as you rest your brow on my bosom
and remember a little
the girl you once were
and how we were whole
you will never know
the joy I feel in your being
no matter where you go
no matter what seeds of death sprout in you
no matter how pregnant with winter
oh my sweet flower of spring
you will never know
how my love for you makes the grains grow.

**Hades**
        (2005)

The simple truth is
I didn't abduct her.
Its true I am almost
as old as her father
but who among gods
counts a few mortal years?

Its true that I probably did
seem powerful to her
the king of the dead
and all that—I don't deny it.

But let's be quite clear
about the power she had–
her skin as delicate as the famous
flower she bent to pluck,
her eyes–have you never
been bewitched by a child's eyes
not yet narrowed by hurt,
open to horizons and possibilities
beyond all you long ago left,
and a smile that invites you to join
in a life that's all laughter and play,
all that in a grown woman's body
riding the swell of first breasts?

Don't you think the sight
and the smell of her
brought me to my knees?
Don't you think my heart stopped
and then thundered off?
Those horses that they say
dragged her away -
the horses of hell -
their hooves were my
terrified heart.

Sure, she was intrigued to see
a powerful king of her father's generation
brought to his knees by her beauty.
Her power, not mine,
rather her power over mine,
seized her.

Informed consent.
You're telling me she didn't know what
she was getting herself into.
That she felt abducted, felt raped
once she had to reckon
with the absolute otherness
of her choice.

And yes. I agree.
There was no informed consent.
For her or for me.
What flared up between us
burned both of our faces away.

She was abducted
of course.
So was I.
But the simple truth is
I didn't do it.

## Hera Speaks
   (1991)

True, there are forces that churn in me,
waves in a great storm at sea, or wind
ripping loose trees, hurling lightning,
pummeling rain. You might think that
these forces can see, that they know where
they're going. You might think that
these forces are blind. You would not be
entirely wrong. True, I was not content to stay
the Great Mother, to pair each year anew
with my son become lover, then sacrifice one
to make room for another. Twenty-five
thousand years, icebound with grief for each
child gone, each lost lover, yet with green
and with flowering love, with open embrace,
greeting each birth.
To love what must die grew difficult.
I grew more than bored with the cycle.
So painfully dull, that repeated exercise
of my own sovereign power, sovereign
over all but the mortal rhythms of life.
Even the greatest goddess is subject to fate.

Gods find repetition
far more interesting than goddesses do:
gods are so technically innovative,
so intrigued with the stage effects,
details, management, a god
can often persuade himself
it's an entirely new story, as he toys
with the mechanics of telling it.
And at heart they are boys: they never tire
of demolition. And this flair for destruction
protects them from grieving, they stand apart
from the mortal world.
I doubt though that the gods will endure
as long as I did. There's a pull in them toward
apocalypse, that strange final dream of an end,
of a mortal-immortal reunion.

Perhaps, over the ages, one or more dreams
did form and disperse among the blind
or seeing forces that churn and guide me.
Perhaps among these was the dream
of a lasting union. A god whose power
could match, might overpower, mine.
You try sole rule for twenty-five thousand years,
see if a few centuries of submission
don't sound diverting to you. It's true,
I did dream of an equal union, an equal
and opposite mate. I also dreamed
of being dominated, humiliated, abandoned.
The blood of twenty-five thousand slain
lover-sons cried out for vindication,
or at least variation.
Even mortal males who lack compassion
tire after a few decades of power. They require
call girls who enact upon them scenes
of humiliating submission, simply to
rejuvenate them to shoulder the burdens of power.

If dreaming I called into being another immortal,
a god who could not die, one who could relieve
the fatigue of my power, one who could change
me from Mother the Awesomely Great
into a merely ridiculous wife,
who can complain about that?
To say Zeus began as a call boy,
a fantasy drawn from my almost infinite
boredom - and grief - would not be entirely
wrong. Power and compassion are a terrible
pair, and I was alone. My wifely jealousy
may seem foolish indeed, but I am free
from the yearly sacrifice of my lover-son.
All that remains of that ancient grief
is the vestigial ceremony of my virginity,
annually restored each year by bathing
in Kanathos spring, that spring of pure water,
not blood. And the innocence which I lose
and regain is simply my ignorance

of domination by the male gods.
No blood guilt is mine. No guilt to be
cleansed only with blood, no
purification rite to bless a fecundity
which consumes and destroys my own
mortal offspring, which again and again
and again destroys what I love,
to make myself fertile again.
As for Zeus, he is no more
touched by my rites or jealousy
than a rutting bull by a flea,
I am free to rage against him powerlessly.
What an indulgence to be jealous
over Zeus, to rage and to fume,
and to leave all the power to him.
It's true I had intended equality,
but he was new to power,
unready to share,
while I was old to it indeed
and grateful to be spared.

The immortal forces dreamed on,
and a god dreamed up "I AM THAT I AM,"
the Great Father God, and in time,
the sacrifice of a son. He managed to make it
a one-time event and cast me as mortal,
the virgin-mother, utterly empty of power
and sin, a pure receptacle to receive
the seed of the potent god.
So peripheral to the salvation drama,
no role for me in the mystery cycle at all
(one of those innovations that so
amuse male gods), all I can do is hold
my dead son (not even lover)
in my helpless and mortal arms.
I am utterly relieved of power,
not even cast as the ridiculous
though challenging wife of the god.
This God needs no woman, neither
mother nor wife, he is the absolute
Father, and I make a charming pieta,

powerless, innocent, all I need do
is weep.

What a treat it has been,
this interlude of the Father.
What a refreshing recess from power.
Mortal females may feel betrayed,
but I can't live for them.
No god or goddess, not one, not one
immortal can dance to a mortal tune.
The forces inside me dream and churn,
power and compassion divide and unite,
the forces dream, but do not assume
that they seek. Neither goodness,
nor holiness, nor meaning -
qualities of much concern to you mortals,
it's true, but we immortals must outlive
your temporal concerns.

## Medea's Son
### (1992)

What can I do to escape my mother's hands?
O my dear brother, I cannot tell. We are lost.
O help us, in god's name, for now we need your help.
Now, now we are close to it. We are trapped by the sword.
                              The Medea, by Euripides


My name is Mermerus, this is my little
brother, Pheres. Our father is Jason, he's
an important man. He divorced us and
our mother, Medea, to marry a beautiful
princess. Of course Mother's mad, but
we're men, we understand about Dad.
Who wouldn't want to marry a princess?
He says our little brothers will be kings
and we'll be their advisers. Mother says
the king is scared of us because people
know that she's foreign and has magical
powers. People talk about how she and
Dad got kicked out of Iolcus, after she
got King Pelias' daughters to cut him
up in a stew. She actually convinced them
that he would leap out of the boiling
cauldron whole and young again, too:
that's how cunning our mother is.

If I were King Creon, I'd be afraid
of my mom, wouldn't you? Then
there's the story of how she helped Father
steal the golden fleece from her people.
After that, she cut her own brother in bits
and tossed him little by little into the sea,
just to slow down her father's pursuit,
knowing he'd need to rescue his
only son's body. Pheres and I study how
Antigone chose to die, rather than leave
her brother unburied. Antigone didn't care
if he was a traitor, if he made war on the
city: he was her brother. That's what we'd

do for each other, Pheres and I. Everyone
has someone they'd do anything for:
our mother would, for our father.

But Mom doesn't want us to be banished,
that's why she says she's sending us
with this beautiful gold gown and diadem
as a present. She's granddaughter of the
Sun: that's who the dress comes from and
why it looks like it's spun out of light.
Funny how I can see it all happening before
it actually does, I guess that's because
I'm a sorceress' son. At first the princess
won't like our coming, we'll watch how
those two adoring puppies, her eyes, keep
flinging themselves at our father again and
again. She won't like how he keeps looking
at us, but when she finally sees the golden
shimmer of the dress, she won't be able to
resist touching it, holding it, beginning to
dance. She'll be in a trance of beauty, a
dazzle of light. We of course won't stay,
we'll hear it from slaves, how the dress
will stick to her skin, how it will burst
into flames, how our mother's beautiful
gift will murder both princess and king.

The slaves will warn us that our mother
plans next to kill us. They'll want to save
us, but they won't have the power. When
Mother approaches with her sharp sword,
her eyes ablaze like the princess's dress,
what can anyone do? Just think of the king
cut up for the cauldron, the brother cut up
for the sea. She conceived and bore us for
this, to make our father suffer as she does.
She'll rob him of sons, as he robbed her of
a husband. Our mother never sees us, she
never sees anyone, only our father - that's
Aphrodite's doing, so people say. Love
is her beautiful gift. So dazzling, they say,

so blinding and bright, no one can resist it,
but if you ask me, it's just like the poison
dress we're bringing the princess. It sticks
to the skin, and it burns. We will die,
Pheres and I, because of this love.
Our father will not arrive in time,
and he will not be able to protect us if
he does, not so long as the slashing sword
of Aphrodite rules our mother's hands.

## Callisto
(1992)


The first time I looked in your eyes, Artemis,
I saw a midwife who slid elbow-deep into
a laboring bear to pull a trapped cub
into life, a huntress who aimed arrows singing
through woods into flesh, a slayer who
plunged her own knife into a deer's throat,
bathed in a spurt of hot blood. I saw
the moon in your eyes, changing, bright,
out of reach, and the river, fresh, cold as ice.
I felt the yelp of the hound with his nose
to the wind, leaping into the rapture of chase.

Answering your call, I chose chastity, not
to relinquish but to actively seek my own
pleasure: to live wild and free, not as prey
but as huntress, stalking more softly than breath,
tracking more intently than cat, aiming
more exactly than eagle: pursuing delight,
I became one among you and your nymphs.

Yet, on the day you walked toward me, slowly,
I became prey, paralyzed by passion as a rabbit is
by fear, wanting to be opened by your eyes,
your fingers, your tongue, your teeth,
letting my own slow gaze slide down
your strong shoulders, graceful arms,
long narrow hands – smooth as carved marble.

On the day you walked toward me, slowly,
the curve of my throat, breast, hip rose
like a cat to meet your caressing eye,
desire seized my whole body, desire
pulled me taut, desire left me limp, languid
as a bowstring snapped by overstretching,
my eyes slaves to your slightest gesture,
my flesh vibrating with need, so that even
the careless fingers of breeze, flicking

from my skin the sweat of the hunt, sent
sharp thrills reverberating through my body.

On the day you walked toward me, slowly,
I became the rose who would never again
be a bud, my petals all spread, their bare
throats curled back to the sky as if knowing
they were soon going to die. How could I not
yearn for a bee who would enter and play
in the midst of this unveiled mystery, one
whose whole buzzing body would plunge,
tumble, roll among fluttering petals, who
would prance, dance, rub, bathe in my pollen,
this fine yellow powder of desire, by which
Aphrodite has laid down her claim?

Yet when you had crossed the slow
distance between us, when your lips,
tongue, fingers, your arms, ribs, soft breasts,
all pressed into mine, your goddess body
a fountain of heat, surrounding, entering,
filling my body, I gasped
at pleasure almost too sweet,
more sweet than the nymphs with their flutes,
more sweet than vanishing twilight reflected
into the lake, more sweet than the chase,
more sweet than the kill. I was a fresco
being painted by you, clay you caressed
into shape, flute in your lips, lyre at your
fingertips: a sobbing child, my oldest
sorrows melted down into beauty by you.

Until my bones and flesh, in sudden protest,
broke the spell. You were alien, you who
had ventured too close to my soul. I tore
free from your grasp, from the joy, from
the love greater than flesh could endure.

Was it then, when I struggled and screamed,
that you dropped your goddess disguise,
ceased to pose as the virgin huntress I loved,

the Lady of wildness and wood?
When the rhapsody of our mutual pleasure
dissolved, you revealed another mask: Zeus,
the Lord among gods, powerful over all others,
unmoved by another's pleasure or pain,
Zeus, who takes what he wants.

I wrestled against your god-force, and
in that fury of tooth and claw, my jaw
strengthened and increased, my muscles
thickened, a heavy pelt grew on my skin.
The stories tell that I was changed into a she-bear later:
when as Artemis you punished my broken
chastity vow, or as Hera, my trespass
against your royal marriage. But I know
it was rage that changed me, rage against you,
Zeus, you who would stoop to steal your precious
god-seed back from my belly and leave me, beast,
bereft even of my human son, until the day
I sought him in the woods, and gazed
for the first time into my own child's face.
Blinded by my wildness, he could not
see the womb he began in, but aimed his
human arrow between my animal eyes. Just
in time to spare him that crime, you transposed
us both to the sky – two bears made entirely
of stars, neither mortal nor god – where we
slowly circle the night, patiently stalking you,
the god, who may tire before we do.

**Ariadne**
(1991)

*for Chris, and for Dick (whose Ariadne she is) as he struggles
back after months of coma following a cerebral aneurysm*


Black sails flap in the strong sea wind.
A mortal woman shrieks from the shore
"Theseus, lover, don't go."

Or the labyrinth tips
the crown of light extinguishes itself
and the thread slips
from the hero's fingers.
"Ariadne, I've lost the thread."

Her marriage with the god comes before, or after,
then before, or after,
again.
As a goddess
she wanders the labyrinth of myth
becomes maze, monster, madness and thread,
guide and sacrifice
killer and killed.
The god comes to claim her around certain corners:
bride of death, mother of death,
rent and torn by her lover-son,
born by her own contracting labyrinth
into death, that labyrinth born of the labyrinth
in which the serpentine myth uncoils and lives.
Meanwhile Theseus living a mortal life: in his skull,
blood blossoms, a weak vessel bulges,
eyes dim and memory wavers.
The crown of light fades.
"Ariadne," he calls
"I'm losing the thread."

And turning a corner, she sees
black sails flap in the strong sea wind
"Theseus, lover, don't go"

a mortal woman wakes on the shore,
alone.

# Medusa
### (2002)

My father resented my golden curls.
He said I had stolen the sun
from my dark-haired brother.

I never knew that he feared my mind, too,
feared all those thoughts that wriggled
and squirmed and sprang
from my young girl's brain -
those fine thoughts of mine
with their bodies that rippled like water,
their tongues of pure flame,
the permanent poison he feared
if a mere glimpse of fang
sang through the symphonic mist
of hissed whispers.

In those days I still dreamed
that within the fond gaze of a male
I could become perfect and whole.
But the boys looked away,
just as my own father had,
as if they really believed
I could turn them to stone.
(a few blind boys did come to play
in my tresses: I turned them
to butter, not stone.)

Later, the girls came to play
in my garden of snakes.
They delighted to stroke
those undulating serpentine bodies.
They delighted to dance
in the lightning flash of sudden tongues.
When the snakes purred and sighed
behind half-closed eyes,
the girls milked the venom
right out of their fangs.

**Eurydice Reluctantly Returns**
(2003)


It's not a job I'd have picked,
this being the soul of their marriage.
I tired quick of trying to stretch
to embrace the mad pace
of two people racing
their different ways
in this headstrong world.
I tired of stretch, contract, stretch,
contract, tired, as the trusting
animals of their bodies grew tired,
tired of being torn apart, forced
back together again and again and again.

I don't think those two even knew
when I died, both of them out there
deliriously drunk on the wild hip-hop
adventure of their individual jab jump jive
raps with the world. I don't think
they even felt the absence
of my barely discernible purr
that once passed from one
to the other of them
not needing even
the touch of their skin.

Listen, death is a quiet place
my whole being here
curled tightly around
nonbeing, petals never
needing to open
so collected, such rest

Deep down
in the world below,
I was perfect
as an unopened bud.
I loved being dead.

There was nothing
I wanted.

Those two
had to come bustling through
with all that upper world
urgency, some kind of emergency,
the two of them suddenly
helping each other, minds falling
back into old familial ways,
so absorbed in the simple truth
of both being here, both being
now with each other, they forgot
to look back. They broke
every rule of the myth.

Can you believe
that they brought me
all the way home?
So damn pleased
with their Orpheus-selves,
humming their cheerful tune
of habitual mutual help,
humming it with such ease,
they echoed original
bliss, they charmed
even Hades again
and Persephone
remembering
tugged at his sleeve.

Those two, the intruders,
those two, the disturbers
of my perfect peace, they
had to forget the whole plot.
They had to completely forget
to look back.
Here I am dragged
into this damned upper world
of trouble again,
and fool that I am,

all I can think is
how sweet their song is,
how much
without knowing
I missed.

## Arachne's Tapestry
### (1992)

All through the long hours of girlhood,
void of laughter and play, void of
rest, aching fingers and wavering
eyes forced to stay at wheel and loom,
spinning, pulling, pushing, tying
purples dyed by my own father's
stained hands, that man so in love
with kings and their colors, who
smiles and bows as he offers me,
a child, to the king's lust, grateful
to have his daughter so royally used,
and later to use me himself, my mother
long dead, and, besides, to murder
a girl-child's soul, carelessly and
for his own pleasure, makes
him feel like a king, or a god.

Before I was six I learned to stay
quiet and hold still. It was Athene
I silently called out for, goddess
strong enough to defend me. How often
I dreamed of her entering the room:
grey-eyed, serene, a single sweep
of her spear delivering me, Athene
hugging my injured girlhood to
her maiden breasts and lean belly,
raising her shield to protect me.
Athene, of course, never came.
Only now has she come, scolding
my wild rashness, my boasting that I
can weave finer cloth than a goddess.
"Let the contest begin," I reply, refusing
to bow or ask her to forgive.

I can easily read the story taking shape
on her loom, even while weaving my
own. At the tapestry's heart, a stunning
celebration of her glory, her olive tree

247

gift to Athens winning her that city's
name; the four corners, chill warnings
to those who dare challenge the gods:
changed to mountain, crane, stork,
changed to stone, forced to do
terrible things to people they love.
All embraced by spreading branches
of her olive tree, her tree of peace.

As I weave, more than ever before,
I pull, twist, tie threads of my rage,
and my pain, into beauty. All my
life, Athene, I have called vainly on you.
Now at last I will show you my story.

I weave Europa, girl-child, wide-eyed
and curious to stroke the flank of the
bull, his body white as poured milk,
spring cloud, fresh snow sleeping
on pine bough, pale glow of
expectant moon, who grazes not
as other bulls do on tough grass,
but reclines and with great lips
and long tongue delicately sips and
caresses deep purple, glistening
gold petals of flowers, so gentle
I giggle and hug him, climb the smooth
curve of his back, safe in knowing
no one has ever wanted to hurt me
until he leaps, sudden and huge, to
the sea, the blade of his leap severing
me from known shore, from my
family, the cold wet splash of terror
on feet, legs, hands, arms - no longer
me, these puppet limbs that recoil
from drowning and cling to the god.

I weave Asterie, already mother of the
goddess Hecate, Zeus in lust grasping
at my mature body as at a prize in a
contest, and I defy him and run,

248

call forth the full power of my long
Titan legs, hurl my own body into the
sea, since I'd sooner drown than suffer
his siege, but he furious with frustration
changes me into a quail, small soft
feathered quarry, now seized in his
eagle talons, now Zeus of the sky
holds open my fragile bird body to his
battering phallus. My bones snap and crack,
muscles and ligaments rip, feathers fly.

Panting Zeus bursts to the summit of desire
as, still and broken, I lie, my limp neck
dangling from his slowly relaxing grip,
until he lets my body drop into the sea.

I weave Leda, soon to be mother of Helen,
thrown to the ground by Zeus the swan,
deafened by the thunder of his wings,
blinded by the snake lightning of his neck,
my arms struck and bruised by his beak until
I can't fight or speak, until I dissolve. Finned
feet stroke and part me like water, white
plumage blazes, as swan-Zeus the
conqueror glides into my harbor, sowing
the seed of the fire that will consume Troy.

I weave Antiope, hypnotized by the
satyr disguise of Zeus, with nimble
little goat hooves that prance and
cavort, a lewd smile on his lips
as he fondles a wooden flute, as his
fingers dance on the flute, teasing a
melody forth to caress my entire
untouchable skin, especially to lick
and tickle my young and unopened
bud, while he, winking, promises
music wilder than this, if I will
allow him to play on my body. Too
dizzy to deny him, I yield my flesh
to the frenzied tune of his touch

stretching me open to ripples
of ever widening pleasure, until
I am left, pregnant with twins,
facing my father's wrath.

I weave Alcmene, hand trembling
as I part the smooth satins that
curtain my bed, to admit
Amphitryon, beloved husband,
who enters and lies with me in the
nakedness of our first night. I
relive this moment again and
again, the curtain opening, the
man like a god. How could I not
know the disguise? As I see the
light fade from my husband's hurt
eyes, as I gasp for life through labor
stretched seven days by Hera's rage,
as I live to see my half-god grown son
go mad and murder his children –
again and again, the curtain opens:
how could I not know the god?

I weave Danaë, locked in first
bloom in my underground prison,
bars so tight only air and rain can
squeeze through, my father crazy in
his need to keep me a virgin, somehow
to defeat the Delphic oracle, not
to die at the hands of my son.
When Zeus does come as gold rain,
I spread open my arms and hands,
loose my bodice, lift my skirt,
allow raindrops to dance on my
ankles and feet - this is the moment
of which the Oracle spoke: for this
god's pleasure, and mine, my father
will die. I lift my face to the rain,
feel the god stream down my eyelids,
cheeks, tongue, feel the god flow
down my throat, breast, belly, thigh.

I writhe on wet earth, my knees shake,
my thirsting fingers spread open
the flower of my girlhood to the
thrust and the pounding of rain,
my hips lift and stretch to receive,
in roaring cascade, the god's need.
I say, let my father die.

I weave Aegina, seemingly unharmed
when the flame of the god licks my
body to hot coals, when the fire of
the god entwines my skin so tightly
I need never again feel cold or alone.
I go willingly with him to Oenone island,
and willingly bear him a child. But where
is Zeus, my burning god of a lover,
when his pleasure is done, and Hera
slips snake poison into the water,
leaving my son with no mother?

I weave Mnemosyne, Memory, Titaness
sleeping nine nights on the ground in the
wondering arms of a shepherd, youth
whose dark eyes and pale skin are softer
than a girl's. I kiss the first gentle fuzz
that covers his chin, I stroke and suck
the wobbly stem of his pleasure into
the thickening trunk of a tree. His huge
pupils hold only me, as he catches his
breath, his hips following at first like
a puppy, then thrusting urgently into the
lead. I have never felt more commanding
than this: crushing innocence like a
flower, summoning lust like a wave,
until I learn my boy lover is but
another disguise for Zeus, so I, the
trifler, am the trifled with. And the
muses, nine daughters of our double
seduction: what mischief will they inspire?

251

I weave Persephone, my maiden eye
caught by a sudden sinuous flash - red,
blue, yellow, black - slithering under bush,
under ground, my child fingers hungry
to touch such vanishing magic, yet
each time I dart forward into the snake's
colorful path, terror jerks my hand back.
It's as if I become a grown woman as I
steady my hand, choose to acquiesce to the
snake's subtle intent, choose to spread
open my thighs to undulations of night, sun,
rose, lake, only to learn it is you, Father -
Zeus - clothed in wild beauty to cheat your
own daughter of choice. Who will be born
from our tryst but my own brother-son,
Dionysos, vine winder, entangler, most
entrancing of gods, he who sips at sweet
ecstasy, and rips apart living flesh.

No more now of Olympic Zeus.
I turn to the glorious deeds of his
brother Poseidon, king of the sea.

I weave Canace, young girl fleeing
the surf of the god, in which I can
hear the pounding, pursuing hooves
of Poseidon the bull, though my own
heart and pulse beat louder still;
gasping for breath, I fling forward
arms, body, legs, until I am seized
by the sea god, the bull, trampled,
stampeded, submerged by wave after
wave of his rutting pleasure. When
finally I rise, unsteady on my feet,
wiping the stinging sea from my
eyes, I can feel the salt come of
the god drip down my thighs.

I weave Iphimedeia, slipping down
to the river Enipeus, to be calmed
by the soft steady murmur of this

river I've loved since my birth, when
sudden arms flood the bank, grasp
my young body, drag me down into
rapids where, thrust up, pulled under
by Poseidon, caught in currents of
his pleasure until nearly drowned, so
that this god for one moment can slake
his immortal thirst, I am robbed.

I weave Theophane, changed
from human to sheep by Poseidon
to conceal me from suitors, so he,
divine ram, can possess me as
animals do, from behind, engendering
my miracle child, golden-fleeced lamb
able to fly and to speak, and who,
taught to abhor his father's greed,
will forfeit his life and his fleece
to save one human being. For this,
the gods, who are not always unjust,
will transform him into a sheep of stars,
and give him a place in their heavens.

I weave Demeter, mother of
undefended Persephone, child
torn from our shared upperworld
by rape, pulled down to the world
below. I roam this childless surface
alone, aimless, while Poseidon's lips
curl with lust as he stalks the once
powerful earth mother, buffeted now
by my own tears, reduced to rending
my own hair and clothes. I change
to a mare, conceal myself among
the Arcadian herd, but Poseidon
appears, rears, thrusts his stallion
sex in, screams and releases a
starburst of seeds only to leave me
with a colt he has sired, this god
who plunders the mother, as his
brother has plundered the child.

I weave a young, lovely Medusa,
refusing all mortal suitors, pleased
and entire in myself, until one day
worshipping at your shrine, Athene,
Poseidon in bird form swoops
down, beak and talons break
into my body, shatter the self
I have known, while you, goddess,
deaf to my cries for protection,
busily devise punishment for
defiling your temple: changing
my hair into snakes, giving me
a face that will turn men to stone.

I weave Melantho, girl so at
home when at sea, that I swim
before walking, hurtle waves with
young dolphins before learning
human play, dive glide jump whirl
among them in sure-bodied synchrony
with their song, long before dancing
to human music. Naturally I am
not afraid, even bold, when a
handsome, half-grown, not yet
known dolphin calf offers a graceful
duet, until he calls on my own
old friends to corral me. I am stunned
by past playmates who nip and
cuff me with once gentle fins, who
join in the gusto of lust as the god's
leaping body crescendos to terrible
sweetness, shattering my trust.

No more for Poseidon, I weave
proud exploits of other gods now.

I weave Isse, little shepherdess girl,
unnerved after weeks of Apollo in
hawk-wings swooping for newborn
lambs, Apollo in lion-skin lunging

for grownup sheep. Night after night
I'm unable to sleep, until Apollo in
herdsman disguise offers to mingle
his goats with my sheep, stand guard
against dangers he's in secret author of,
even massage and soothe my taut
muscles to sleep. He pauses while I,
relaxing at last, swoon into grateful
half-sleep. I hardly know he peels
my protective fingers away, spreading
open before him my exhausted body.

I weave Erigone, born among
grapes and oak barrels of wine,
dancing the harvest from earliest
girlhood, barefooted, skirt bunched
and raised, stamping and crushing
ripe grapes free from their skins.
But now I also grow ripe, and
Dionysos now dwells in the grape.
These are his dark juices that lick
between my toes, clasp my ankles,
splash up my thighs, until, gripping
my waist with god force, Dionysos
pulls me down into the bruised wet
sweet flesh of the grapes, where,
trampled and crushed as they are,
I too am forced free of my skin.

I weave Philyra, incited by Cronus'
glance, most powerful of gods
who deigns to desire my trifling self.
My cheeks flame, my thighs melt,
my trembling legs barely support me
as I touch the silk of his stallion nose,
stroke his throat, withers, flank,
fondle his huge swollen penis, the
greatness of which in delirious glory
I stretch and tear to receive, until
my aunt, his wife, appears. Hunched
and hidden, I watch my belly swell

with the half-horse monster I've made.
When Zeus takes power from Cronus,
dethroned, I ask mercy of him:
make me into a tree. Spare me
knowing that my monster-child,
wise and gentle Chiron, the greatest
of healers, will receive a wound
even he cannot heal. Spare me
knowing that my son, an immortal,
will pay with permanent pain
for my one moment of pleasure.

The final scene, then – Philyron,
mother of the centaur Chiron,
begging to be changed to a tree,
spared eyes to see her suffering
child. With my tapestry almost
completed, I see terrified Europa
ride the white bull, Asterie caught
by the eagle, Leda subdued by
the swan, Antiope beguiled by
the satyr, Alcmene by her own
husband's likeness, Danaë by
gold rain, Aegina by flame,
Mnemosyne by shepherd boy,
Persephone by snake. I see Canace
terrorized by the bull, Iphimedeia
by the river, Theophane by the ram,
Demeter by the stallion, Melantho
by dolphin, Medusa by bird. I see
Isse deceived by herdsman,
Erigone by grapes, Philyron by
stallion. All that I meant to reveal
to Athene, I see, while my fingers,
graceful from habit, go on weaving
the final edge with its delicate
border of ivy and flowers,
then stitch the last narrow hem.

Athene sees only that I have
outdone her: she rips the tapestry

from my loom, tears it to rags,
splits open the frame, pries off
the shuttle, cracks hard wood
against my mortal forehead. Skull
fractured, blood streaking my face -
nothing to live for - I meet the
grey eyes. "Goddess," I say,
" I concede. Yours is the greater gift,
you who destroy finer cloth than you
weave." I fasten a noose of fine
purple around my own neck, throw
the twisted strands over the high
branch of a tree, tighten and swing,
almost free, when Athene stops me,
cries "You'll hang all right, but alive:
you and your family, on and on into
the last generation, you'll hang and
you'll weave." She splashes juice
of strange-smelling herbs from Hecate,
and I'm not me anymore, not dead
either, suddenly shrinking and
changing: head, arms, legs sucked
into my tiny belly, soft skin hardening,
fingers scrawny and wriggling, stuck
to my sides: they continue to weave.
My fingers, now legs, press and
attach a thin sticky almost invisible
thread to the noose, (now a vast rope,
many times thicker than I am). My
fingers leap off, leave me dangling in
air from this thread spinning forth
from my body. I wait for wind
to whisk me to some random branch,
to define the new edge of my loom.

No challenge now to the goddess:
I weave and reweave my identical
web, suspend it in air, invisible, wait
for a wild winged creature to come,
collide, stick; wait for its fight for
escape, for its terrified beating of

wing, to make it more firmly adhere,
to make the web quiver, summoning
me to desire. Finger-walking across
the rippling expanse of web, immune
to its glue, I greet the new guest
with the poisonous kiss of desire,
so that, motionless but awake, you
can watch while I, punished by
Athene and made almost a god,
suck the sweet life from your body.

# Gods in Our Midst

## Orpheus
### (1966)

I too, Lazarus, I came again.

I out of the gaping, man-eating
underworld gates once strode,
my soul in death-white swathing
and suffocating, prayer
the only breath it could inspire.
But holding somehow, knowing that below
in darker darkness, and with lesser breath,
slowly, slower than stars through blackness,
came my regained Eurydice from Hades,
now her dwelling place
this whole chipped moment of eternity
since last we, living both, embraced.

Time spent apart, a jagged corner chiseled
from our love's crystal palace, polished
to prism fineness by Lethe's quiet art,
divides the light, distorts the images,
so that I, seemingly among the living,
turn back to look at my Eurydice
while she in darkness, ready to emerge,
will not now, never will be seen.

So I too, Lazarus, I came again.
For which, as is well-known,
even among the wheezing, dim-eyed Fates,
I am not grateful, burn no incense,
sing no pious songs
to the indulgent, permanent, ambrosia-eating Gods.

## Hephaestus at the High School Reunion
### (1993)

Gregory Smith, you remember him,
the guy in the wheelchair. He's

over there, almost unchanged:
the same high forehead,
flushed cheeks,
deep-set eyes,
the same hooked,
shriveled hands,
dangled legs,
the only change
is the need in his eyes,
which is gone; that, and
the creepy feeling we got
when he used to talk about sex.

Now he's husband, father,
provider and flourishing artist.
There's nothing he needs from us now,
except maybe
to show us he no longer needs:
how he takes this twisted truth of his body,
this, and the turned backs of our gaze, the wince
when our eyes accidentally slip across his,
he takes it, he takes it all in,
he bites down on his brush
and he paints.

## On Meeting a Man You Could Trust
(1993)

Mountain of a man, with a mood as thick
and musky as the mane of a lion, with a mind
that could seize and hold your heart
like a cub in the mouth of its mother.
The first time you looked in his eyes,
snared in his aura as surely as a fish is
in the fierce and undulating arms
            of an anemone,
even if you had never given yourself
fully to any other man, you chose
to spread open your soul before him,
which he devoured with such relish,
and gave back so entirely intact,

that for the rest of your life
you would never forget
that for that one moment at least
you had been touched by a god.

## Cruising in the Getty Sculpture Garden
(1993)

This youth who basks naked
at poolside, how carelessly
he leans back, raises his face,
arches his throat, lets his legs ease
onto the contoured rock,
how casually he spreads open
his thighs as he offers his cock
to the sun's dazzling mouth.

## Transforming Jim
(1993)

Jim enters, stage left. In the
pride of his manhood, he struts,
faded levis slung on angular hips,
cotton shirt spanning the haughty
masculinity of his chest.
The performance begins:
delicately drawing eyebrows,
lightly stroking eyeliner,
lining and painting the softness
and fullness of lips, black brassiere
with soft padding, wig of flaming
red curls, black satin scant
dress. The feline inclination
of ankle, thigh, calf,
as he slides into each
elegant sinuous pump.
The swing of his hips,
the exuberance that comes
naturally, the liquidity, as he
gushes forth, transformed into she,
all in memory of Ellie May,

his first (now dead)
drag queen friend.

## On my way to the Wedding of two Divorced Friends
    (1993)

Startled by the silence, trying
the key again, engine not stirring.
Headlights accidentally on,
broad daylight. (More and more
now, memory stalls, more
troublesome than when the car does,
no Triple-A to be called on.)
Good fortune, though, to be
parked on a hill, able to coast as if
back to girlhood: my first used car,
sixty-six Plymouth Valiant,
vintage year, famed slant-six engine
able to soften the gaze of any mechanic
whose eyes might stray under the hood.
Releasing the handbrake, steering
into the street, shifting to second,
slowly lifting the clutch, no lurch
of the old Valiant bursting to life, just
the smooth purr of the Honda engine
stretching awake, and the joy of a thing
given back. As I turn the corner,
a man with one leg bicycles past.

## Sisyphus
    (2007)

Everyone knew
I was in love with that rock.
The hard reality of it—
as I'd lean all I could muster
of muscle and sweat
and press forward
and upward,  shouldering
the elemental opposition of it,
legs, arms, buttocks, chest

against gravity, pressed
into cool and unyielding rock.
We were intimate
in a way I have never been
with anything living,  its
weight so close to my will.

And when we reached the top
and it slipped from me
into free fall, veered
in a wild avalanche of one
all the way down the hill,
absence and distance were
all I could feel until
it tumbled still.

Then at the bottom
I could
take it into my arms again
and be whole.

### Narcissus's Pond
(2008)

Whatever the others say, you and I know
that when Narcissus saw his reflection

he knew he was beautiful and good
and he learned how to love.

So what if it killed him?
The others might say

it was all his reflection,
but we know

I played a part.
My presence,

the way the mud at my bottom
lay still–

the clear, unrippled surface I gave him.
I had learned

not to restlessly search for my own
yearned-after reflection, to lie still, to love

the unreflective surface of the actual world.
I did nothing.

I waited—
but I gave him

what he needed
so that when he saw

what he so deeply loved
in my water,  I saw

my reflection
in him.

**Orpheus in the Underworld**
    (2007)

From down here
how differently
it all looks.

Ah Eurydice
you who were never "my" Eurydice
here among shadows and smoke
you become your own.

And I too
torn into pieces and strewn
in the fields where perhaps
what was once my separate being
helps new life to grow
(whether we speak of my flesh
or my songs—it's all the same now)

I too who perhaps
was never my own
have learned I belong.

We walk here,
detached and together,
shadows and smoke,
fall softly
into and out of each other,
commingle and
come apart.

Sometimes
you walk ahead,
sometimes
you walk behind.
It doesn't matter here
whether we look
forward or back,
this way or that.

## Mythological Notes
## (based on Crowell's Handbook of Classical Mythology by Edward Tripp)

Aphrodite. A goddess of erotic love.

Arachne. A young Lydian woman adept at weaving, famous for her skill at the loom. She boasted that she would not hesitate to pit her skill against that of Athene, goddess of crafts. Athene visited in the form of an old woman to warn the girl of the dangers of her presumption. When Arachne scorned her, the goddess revealed herself and the contest began. Athene wove legends of humans punished by the gods for arrogance. Arachne countered by flawlessly depicting a few scandals involving the gods. Athene had been merely annoyed at the girl's boasts, but when she saw her skill was in fact equal to her own, she flew in a rage, tore up the tapestry and beat the girl. Arachne tried to hang herself, but the goddess changed her into a spider, with her talent for spinning unimpaired. Ovid, in Metamorphoses, gives a detailed description of Arachne's tapestry, based on mythical scandals probably creatively elaborated by him. (My poem is based on Ovid's tale, taking even further liberties to elaborate the stories, and also changing the gods and goddesses names back from those of the Roman to those of the Greeks.)

Ariadne. Daughter of Minos, king of Crete. When Theseus came to Crete with other intended victims of the Minotaur, Ariadne fell in love and helped him escape from the Labyrinth after he killed the monster. As he promised, he took her with him, but later left her on the island of Dia. Accounts differ: he may have deserted her, or Dionysos may have stolen her. She may have committed suicide, or married Dionysos (or his priest). Or Theseus may have been carried away by storms, leaving Ariadne to die of grief on Cyprus. In some accounts she had several children by Dionysos. Most modern authorities believe Ariadne was not merely a mortal character of mythology but a Cretan goddess, worshipped in several widely scattered parts of the ancient world.

Artemis. A virgin goddess of childbirth and of wild animals. Despite her reputation as the chaste huntress, most scholars agree she was originally a cult patroness of all living things, animal and human, a mother-goddess similar to the Minoan "Lady of the Wild Things." At her chief cult center, her priestesses probably dressed as bears, and the bear Callisto may have been a local form of Artemis herself. Among the Greeks she became, paradoxically, a virgin goddess of childbirth. Her association with the moon was widespread.

Athene. The virgin goddess of arts, crafts, and war, and the patroness of the city of Athens. She was often depicted as a tall, stately woman wearing a crested helmet and often carrying a spear and shield. She was born from Zeus' head, wearing full armor (Zeus had swallowed her mother out of fear that his offspring might overthrow him, as he overthrew his own father.) She was associated with courage and ingenuity, and in later times with wisdom. The owl was her bird.

Callisto. A favorite of Artemis. Some call her a nymph, others a mortal. Some say that she had taken vows of chastity. Zeus saw her alone in the woods, disguised himself as Artemis, gained her confidence, then took advantage. Some say Zeus changed her to a bear to hide his embarrassment when Hera spied on them, others say Hera did it out of jealousy, or Artemis as punishment for breaking her vows. There are various accounts of Callisto's end: one is that Artemis shot her while hunting and that Zeus rescued his baby Arcas from her womb and gave it to his mother to bring up. Another is that Arcas, grown to manhood, saw the bear and shot at it, or was about to shoot at it. Zeus immortalized Callisto by transporting her to the stars as the constellation Arctos, the Great Bear. Then or later Arcas became the nearby constellation Arctophylax, which appears to be guarding the Bear. Hera, still jealous, made sure Callisto could not enter the realm of her old nurse, the sea-goddess Tethys and her husband, Oceanus. So Callisto does not set like other constellations, but is doomed to revolve ceaselessly around the North Star.

Demeter. Ancient goddess of corn or of the earth and its fertility in general. She presided over crops, and grains in particular. By Zeus, she had a daughter, Persephone. One day Hades, brother of Zeus, ruler of the Underworld, fell in love with Persephone. Zeus approved the marriage and, knowing Demeter would not, suggested that Hades abduct Persephone. Zeus helped by inducing Ge (even more ancient earth goddess) to send up hosts of lovely flowers to attract the girl and her companions. Demeter wandered and searched and finally learned from Helius (god of the sun) what happened. She wandered the earth in human form, caring nothing for her appearance. While passing through Arcadia, she changed herself into a mare to try to elude Poseidon (god of the sea) who tried to rape her. Not fooled, Poseidon became a stallion and mounted her. She bore Arion, a remarkable horse. In another story, she traveled in the guise of an old woman, and became the nurse of a child who she tried to make immortal by anointing him with ambrosia and laying him to sleep in the embers of the fire. But the mother spied on her, and, horrified at what she saw, cried out in alarm. Demeter brought famine on the earth for an entire year. When reunited with Persephone, she learned that Persephone had tasted the food of Hades, which meant that she must spend at least a third of each year in the underworld. With pressure from Zeus, and Persephone returned to her for two-thirds of each year, Demeter relented and allowed grain to grow once again.

Dionysos. A Greek god of wine, and of vegetation in general, also known as Bacchus. According to the Orphic account, Zeus (in the form of a snake) lay with Persephone, and the resulting child was sometimes identified with Dionysos. Thanks to Hera's jealousy, the child was torn apart and eaten, but his heart was saved. Zeus swallowed it, and tricked a woman, Semele, into giving birth to Dionysos a second time. Worshippers of Dionysos, wearing animal skins and carrying poles twined with ivy and grapevines, participated in orgiastic rites; the women suckled kids or fawns, and sometimes tore them apart with their bare hands and ritually ate them. Sexual license may also have been part of the rites.

Eurydice. A Thracian nymph who married Orpheus but died of snakebite. Orpheus was allowed to bring her back from Hades, provided he not look at her on the way. Unable to bear the strain, he turned to look and she was lost to him forever.

Hades. God of the Underworld, where he preferred to stay, leaving it only once. Having fallen in love with Persephone, he carried her off by force, with Zeus' blessing. Emerging from the earth in his carriage, he snatched the girl while she picked flowers and carried her down to his home. Eventually Demeter forced Zeus to order that the stolen bride be returned. In the meantime, Hades forced or induced Persephone to eat a pomegranate seed. This meant she would have to spend four to sixth months every year with him.

Hephaestus. A god of fire and metalworking, Hephaestus was a son of Zeus and Hera. He was born lame, and Hera threw him out of heaven in disgust. He became a master artisan of infinite ingenuity and artistic gifts.

Hera. A goddess of marriage and childbirth, queen of heaven. Much of Hera's time was spent persecuting her husband's innumerable mistresses and their children. Many scholars believe Hera was originally, like so many other pre-Hellenic goddesses, a patroness of the fertility of the earth. There are strong indications she governed the lives of cattle and flocks, and was connected in cult with crops and flowers. As such, one might speculatively connect her with myths of the great mother whose son-lover is sacrificed each year so that crops can again grow (much as Persephone is sacrificed in the later Patriarchal myths.)

Leda. Daughter of Aeotolian king. Visited by Zeus in the form of a swan. By most accounts, Helen of Troy was born of that union.

Medea. Daughter of Aeëtes, king of Colchis. She was a priestess of Hecate, goddess of the underworld, and so able to work miracles for both good and evil. In this convoluted story, the goddess Hera was angry at King Pelias of Iolcus, and plotted to punish him through Medea. So she arranged for Jason and the Argonauts to sail to Colchis to steal the golden fleece. With Aphrodite's help, Hera caused Medea to fall hopelessly in love with Jason. When Jason promised to marry her, Medea not only helped him to steal the fleece from her people, but helped murder her brother Apsyrtus, then tossed pieces of his dismembered body into the sea from the ship to delay pursuit (while the Colchians rescued the pieces for burial). On their return to Iolcus, Medea not only persuaded Pelias' daughters that she could restore their father's youth, but that they should kill him, chop him up, and throw the pieces in a pot. When Pelias did not emerge rejuvenated, the Argonauts took over the city. Hera's punishment of King Pelias was complete. Later, Jason and Medea moved to Corinth, lived together ten years, and had two sons. Jason was seen as a hero, but Medea was feared as a barbarian sorceress. Creon, King of Corinth, offered his daughter as wife to Jason. Medea, threatened with banishment as well as divorce, reminded Jason of her former help to him, without avail. Enraged, she pretended to submit, and sent her sons to the palace bearing a wedding gift for the princess. When the bride put it on, it burst into unquenchable flame, killing her and her father (who came to her aid) as well. When the Corinthians stormed Medea's house, she escaped in a chariot drawn by winged dragons, a gift from her grandfather Helius (god of the sun). Accounts differ as to the sons: they were stoned to death by the Corinthians, or Medea herself killed them.

Medusa. In late versions of the myth, a beautiful maiden who incurred the enmity of Athena. Athena turned Medusa's lovely hair into serpents and made her face so hideous that a glimpse of it would turn men to stone.

Orpheus. A Thracian minstrel so adept at music that his playing and singing charmed wild animals and caused stones and trees to follow him. After his wife Eurydice died, he descended into the underworld where he sang and played so movingly that the spirits came in hordes to listen, the damned forgot their labors, and even the cold hearts of Hades and Persephone were melted. They granted his plea that he take Eurydice back with him, provided he not look at her until they reached home. He led her to the entrance of the underworld. Then, overcome with fear she might not be following, he turned to look. She instantly faded away.

Persephone. A goddess of the Underworld. She was the only child of Zeus and Demeter. Carried off by Hades (with her return to earth, and the consequent sprouting of crops in the spring, after the seed had remained in the ground all winter, was celebrated in rites shared by mother and daughter, notably the Eleusinian mysteries. In the rape story, Persephone was the unwilling victim torn from her mother. But although she spent two thirds of each year on earth, there are no myths about her stay there. Apart from the tales of rape and rites of return, myths always deal with her as the dread goddess of the Underworld. Although the two sides of Persephone's character may seem contradictory today (and may result from fusion of different myths), they did not appear so to the early Greeks. The seeds of the crops on which their lives depended were, like their dead, buried in the earth, but they came up again each spring. In an Orphic variant, Persephone was seduced by Zeus and gave birth to Dionysos.

Poseidon. A god of the sea, earthquakes, and horses. Like other sea-deities, Poseidon had the power of changing his shape, and seems to have used it in his various seductions. He was depicted with a trident: a three-pronged fish-spear.

Sisyphus. A king of Corinth who committed an unspecified impious act for which as punishment he had to spend eternity in a futile attempt to push an enormous boulder to the top of a steep hill; nearing the top the stone was fated always to roll down again. The most usual reason given for this punishment was that Sisyphus informed the river god Asopus that it was Zeus who carried off his daughter Aegina.

Theseus. Son either of Aegeus, King of Athens, or of the god Poseidon. One of seven youths and seven girls sent as tribute to Crete as food for the Minotaur. The Minotaur was a monster with a bull's head on a man's body kept in the Labyrinth, a mazelike prison from which no one could ever find his way out. Ariadne, daughter of the king of Crete, fell in love with Theseus and gave him a large ball of thread to unwind as he made his way into the maze. After killing the monster, he followed the thread back to the entrance. When he left Crete, Theseus took Ariadne with him, only to be separated later when he abandoned her, or was blown away by a storm, or when she was stolen by Dionysos.

Titans. Very ancient deities, firstborn children of Uranus and Ge. The youngest Titan, Chronus, plotted with his mother to rebel and usurp his father's rule. Later his own son Zeus overthrew him.

Zeus. Ruler of the Olympian gods. He was incessantly involved in seductions of goddesses, nymphs, and mortal women. Zeus sent the rain to fertilize the earth, and also governed the affairs of gods and men, especially punishing mortals for arrogating to themselves divine prerogatives. Zeus began as and forever remained a god of the sky and all its phenomena: bright depths of the clear sky, clouds, thunderbolt, rain.

# I Want To Tell You How Beautiful You Are:
# The Real Women Poems
# (1997-1998)

The Real Women poems were composed as companion poems to the Real Women sculptures by T.J. Dixon. These sculptures, commissioned by Dr. Barbara Levy as part of a dream midwifed by Dr. Donna Brooks and Cathy Conheim, seek to open our eyes and hearts to the diverse beauty of women. Thirteen women (none of us professional models) of various ages, shapes and ethnicities, posed for the sculptures.

For more information on the Real Women Project, please visit www. realwomenproject.org.

Special thanks to T.J. Dixon and James Nelson for their generous permission to use their photographs of their sculptures without charge. For more information about their work, please visit www.n2.net/tjdixon.

## Every Woman Deserves a Poem

I want to tell you how beautiful you are
in such a true and unforgettable way
that you will never doubt it again.
It will be as though through the lens of the poem
you will suddenly see: yourself, truly
the whole of you, naked.

It will be as though you are walking alone
in the woods when a great blue heron lifts
into the air, or a single wild orchid blooms,
or the moon shines down on still water,
and it is enough.
Your heart stops.
You are left
grateful, simply for being alive.

It will be your own beauty this time
taking you so suddenly and by surprise,
the mysterious beauty of your entire life
carefully inscribed in your body.

It will be as though the poem becomes
your dream lover, caresses your skin
with absolute tenderness, lights up
with it's touch every cell in your body,
enters you with a gasp of astonished desire,
plunges deep into the secret
at the center of who you are.

**Estelle at 75**

Though she grasps the fixed surface
upon which she rests
with solid affection, though her left sole
plants itself firmly enough on the ground,
still her shoulders lift as if
with a secret knowledge of wings,
while her right thigh stretches, her right calf
dances and sings, her right ankle
dips its delighted toes into terror and temptation,
the whirling alluring waters of the unknown.

Though her two legs have lived side by side
all her life, the right has its own special way
of touching, speaking, beseeching the left,
as if to discover afresh
that mirror-image opposite twin.
Her right leg peeks out like a playful kitten,
a supple snake about to shimmy up a tall vine,
a child whose toe stretches just beyond the edge
of the world that she's come to love.

But her love of the ordinary keeps her left foot
pressed down, the restless whole of her held
by her hands to this spot, as a boat is held back
by its rope to the shore of the pulsating sea.
One can almost brush up against her invisible wings -
silk-smooth and nuzzling the breeze -
the wings of a butterfly poised on a flower to drink.

## River at 50

In her pain, she curls up into herself
as though loss has helped her to know herself
newborn and naked, again:
an infant without any mother,
a snail without any shell,
a bud still too frightened to flower.

## Deb at 44

Exulting in every ounce of her flesh, Deb lets
her sensuous shoulders and arms sing their own
brash song of delight at being present just as she is,
right here, right now, right along with everybody else.
Her foot flirts outrageously with the entire room,
and she leans back her head and allows
the rapture of her laughter to rise to the rafters,
she allows the pleasure of her presence to radiate out
from this unbridled body of hers, as loaded
with roundness and ripeness as a peach tree
in August, sinfully rich as whipped cream
on a chocolate mousse, soft as a trampoline
bounced on by feather pillows. Deb's laughter
gives "voluptuous" back its good name.

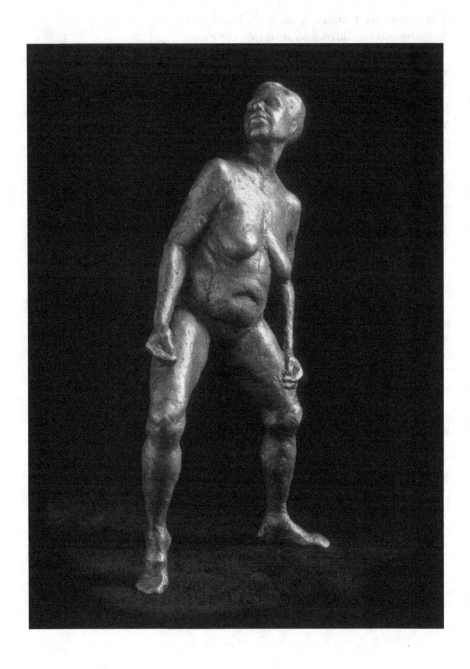

## Tabor at 59

Tabor is ready, whatever life asks.
Her feet will not miss a beat.
The unfaltering aim of her gaze,
the lift of her chin,
the pride in the bones of her cheeks
all announce that
this woman's dance will not end.

Her belly has been a taut dome
over the head of that holy of holies, new life.
A dome whose design could outshine
even the Taj Mahal, and all the seven
wonders of the world (if the truth be told).
This belly is not afraid of a furrow or fold.

Nor is her tunnel of love and of birth
ashamed of itself, of the hidden
muscles that hold and give forth
the loves of a woman's whole life.

Nor do her breasts scorn the fullness
that makes them sag, her breasts
that need climb no mountain to gaze
upon promised land. They have been
the mountain, they have been the land
overflowing with milk and with honey.

She will dance on and on.

## Zona at 33

As the prizewinning rider and horse become one
in the practiced precision of jumps,
so Zona rides astride earth itself,
her warrior stance balanced and sure,
her feet and legs steady above
the galloping, pivoting ground.

But the air into which she looks up
is a whole other element
beneath which her powerful spine arches back
with a whisper, like a reed or a stalk.

In the vast and voluminous air her bare throat
yields to the kiss of a breeze
and one hand relaxes her martial grip,
and one hand touches her hair and her face
as curiously as a lover's hand might
that yearns to open her life to surprise:
sudden danger and wonders
that fall from the skies.

## Kären at 35

Child of mine,
who will you be?
Come out of my body
to me, to me.

At the border between one life and two,
Kären rocks, one hand steady
on the back of her own trusted leg,
one lightly at rest on the globe
that has recreated its shape in her belly.
Beneath the bulge of a whole other world
her feet feel at home on the ground,
find their way through invisible
fields of force as if through a song.

Child of mine,
who will you be?
Come out of my body
to me, to me.

## Lily at 14

Lily lies on the earth more lightly than morning,
open to the newness of this dawning day.
Her young breasts and thighs soften, they sigh
over the lost angularity of her body.
Blood weaves a lullaby into her womb,
teaching her to dance with the moon,
to ebb and to flow with the seasons, with tides.
A woman's hand cradles her head.
A woman's hand on her diaphragm
rises and falls with the rhythms of breath.
A woman's leg stretches luxuriously out from her hip,
but somewhere in her girlhood, a child's foot
tucks itself in under her knee, as if seeking
shelter within the woman she is becoming.

## Chris at 66

She holds herself close. Her limbs
interweave to form a safe nest
of ankles and wrists, with
a solid embankment of knees.
She stretches her arms
into the actual shape of her body
with the delight of a child
who wakes each morning
amazed at the joy
of her own trusted touch: arm,
ankle, calf, fingertip, wrist.
She holds herself close.

Above the safe nest of her body
she holds her gaze steady, sees
into the distance as far as she can.
Far beyond the confines of this nest,
this flower of only a moment,
she sees the universe, vast
and unknown. And she trusts it,
for better or worse,
as she trusts her own body.

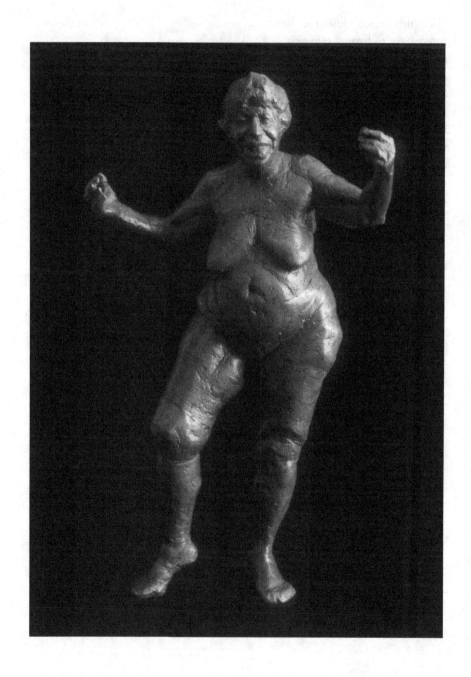

## Elsie at 73

Here she is, folks. This is Elsie.
This is her body, her breasts,
her arms open wide,
and ready to give you
the world's most magnificent hug.

Her hug is a big hug.
She does not apologize
for the space it takes up.
There's a lifetime of love
saved up in her, in her body.
Her hug can lift you and shake you
and take you all the way
to a moment of paradise,
to a place where the world
is made out of safety and love.
You may be afraid to go there,
and Elsie can understand why.
She's known her own devastation,
but her arms open wide just the same.
This is Elsie, folks. Who wants a hug?

**Beverly at 51**

Beverly's belly, chest, breast
and absence of breast
lean into the future with love.
Love lifts her chin
like the prow of a ship parting waves;
love honors the place
where one of her breasts
no longer is. All that her lost
nIpple once yearned to give
in the way of pleasure and sustenance
lives. When Bev hears the cries
of women who suffer as she did,
spirit milk from her spirit breast overflows
through her voice, hands, eyes -
She welcomes, listens, witnesses,
cries, laughs, encourages, hugs.
As a new mother rides the swell
and the spill of the milk in her breasts,
rising to her baby's cries, so Bev rides
the same flood of kindness inside her
that keeps her so keenly alive.

## Julianna at 27 with Iris Roxanna at 2

Iris Roxanna relaxes
in the pillow world
of her mother's middle,
in this pillow world
that ripples and breathes.

Beat by beat
the young drum
of Irls Roxanna's heart
follows her mother's lead,
as she studies the fine art of love.

Julianna, her mother,
lives in two worlds.
In the world of weapons and war
she stands still and strong,
poised to protect.
In the world of pillows and song,
her belly and breasts
make the whole world seem
free from harm.

Though in time truth will intrude
on their magical world,
love will still
reverberate here:
stronger and sweeter
than fear.

298

**Kathy at 38**

She hesitates.
Her foot lingers,
as if sharing secrets
with dew drops
that gather and whisper
among stalks of grass.
Her fingers pause
to count stars.
Above the thin
filament of her body,
her head flickers
like the flame of a candle.
Her thoughts bend and sway
with the breeze.

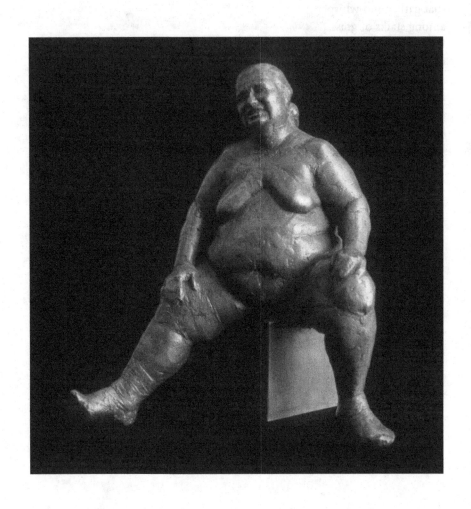

## Wendy at 45

Wendy's right foot stretches out and lets go,
tilts on its heel, waggles a toe. Her toes
are on holiday now, children set free
to bask in the gaze of the sculptor
who dances and sings the grand rounds of her body.

Wendy basks in the laughter of children at play,
invisible children who climb and fall down
on the mounds and mounds, the mountains of her.
They snuggle up into her teddy-bear warmth,
hang on the limbs and the lap of her story,
and leap down again to dance all around her.

They are drawn without knowing
to her great goddess shape, this full
fertile figure our ancestors sculpted
in honor and worship and praise.

# The Boy Who Delights in the World:

Poems With Sculpture

In 1991 rheumatoid arthritis forced Dr. Donna Brooks to retire early from her career as a gynecological surgeon. I composed *Her Hands* for the retirement party. Donna's sculpture teacher T.J. Dixon made a sculpture of Donna's hands to keep the poem company.

When Donna Brooks and her partner Cathy Conheim raised funds to install two sculptures, *The Woman Who Holds Herself* by T.J. Dixon and *The Boy Who Delights in the World* by Donna Brooks at Woman's Medical College hospital, they invited me to compose poems to go with those sculptures.

The poem *Casualties* accompanies larger-than-life bronze figures by T.J. Dixon and James Nelson, commissioned for Clemson University by the class of 1944. The quote at the beginning of the poem is from one of the alumni. The entire graduating class signed up for the war together.

*The Generations at Play* was composed to go with five life-size bronze figures by Dixon and Nelson installed in a fountain at the Beach development in Myrtle Beach, South Carolina.

*Self-Defense,, Ready to Fire* , and *The Man in the Moon* accompany sculptures by Dixon and Nelson in private collections. *The Girl who Holds the World* goes with a sculpture by Donna Brooks in a private collection.

The poem *Dr. June Klinghoffer* accompanies a life-size sculpture of Dr. Klinghoffer by Dixon and Nelson commissioned by Allegheny University (which absorbed Women's Medical College) and installed at Medical College of Pennsylvania Hospital (successor to Women's Medical College Hospital).

*The Wall of Remembrance* goes with an AIDS memorial garden and 7-foot bronze sculpture by Dixon and Nelson.

For years of joyful collaboration and for permission to use photographs of the sculptures without charge, I offer my deepest gratitude to T.J. Dixon, James Nelson, Cathy Conheim and Donna Brooks. The photographs that accompany *Her Hands, The Boy Who Delights in the World*, and *The Girl Who Holds the World* are by Cathy Conheim; all other sculpture photographs are by T.J. Dixon and James Nelson.

## Her Hands

*For Dr. Donna Brooks on the occasion of her retirement*
*with love and friendship from River and Chris*
*September 27, 1991*

They have reached deeply
into the innermost mysteries of the flesh,
unflinchingly cut through living skin and bone,
moved muscles, loosened ligaments,
and calmed the storming panic of the blood.

They have reached deep
inside the mysteries of life
inside the temple of the god, of flesh,
the great replenisher.
These hands have held and bent life
to their dreams, and bid flesh mend
along their careful seams.

These hands have spanned
as few have ever done
both intellect's precise technology—
that views in icy light
the body's most impersonal geometry
and so manipulates, with gestures
sure, detached, and right—
and heart's astonished reverence—
whose subtle fingers meet
and are transformed by
each rare soul embodied in a flesh
uniquely strange, a flake of
human snow, no two alike.

These hands have suffered, and may suffer more
a crippling pain, the flesh god's shadow side.
Lifelong, they strive to limit and contain
the shadow of their god:
these hands know well
that flesh, the great replenisher,
is also mother of decay.
As healer and as sufferer, these hands
do wrestle with the god they love.
These hands do wrestle with the god of life.

## The Woman Who Holds Herself
(1993)

She has not stopped truth
in its game of molecular chairs.
She is only a nesting, of stone.
The long dance she is made of
will leap, stretch, swirl
the wrists of her being again.
    But for now,
body and world wrapped tight
around the sinew of her arm,
she holds all she has ever loved
still, poised above ankles
of seemingly permanent bronze,
while the music of earth plays on.
And she rides these waves
we call home, these waves
we call sweet, bitter home.

## The Boy Who Delights in the World
(1993)

What exists for this boy
inside his own skin
is no more his
than what falls to him
out of the sky.
Light, leaf, water, snow,
brush of breeze or of wing.
He fills his eyes with
the rapture of things.
Grasshopper, puddle, toad, worm,
icicle, butterfly, cloud.
Your own awkward
elbows may no longer recall
this child of first seeing, this fawn
reverberating in a forest of rain.
But your clear heart, green, craves
his absolute beauty of being.
Propped on pure presence, he
seizes your hand, becomes
a still wind
in which the startled
star of your soul
slowly opens.

**Casualties**
   (1996)


*"How can I make you understand? We were boys, mere boys, and then the war came and half of us were dead."*

Just behind this thin veil of time
our boyhoods leapt into history,
trusting, and so eager
you could weep.

The helmets and boots we put on—will we ever
really take them off? Peacetime can paint
tender scenes across the silk veil of time
and we can try not to look

through this insubstantial veil
into the glare of searchlights, the blizzard
of bullets and shells, pure terror inducting us
again and again into a world all war.

We can try not to speak too loudly,
not to step too heavily,
not to disturb the slight veil,
nor lift, nor look behind . . .and for our effort,

we find ourselves changed into tired old men,
the fine veil into a fortified wall,
behind which our boyhoods still wait,
unopened as buds caught by frost, as
colts that never discovered their gait.

**The Generations at Play**
   (1993)

Listen, I will tell you a secret. The generations–
wherever they play, there is a hidden,
invisible fountain. It is the place
that replenishes luck,
and anyone falls in that fountain of love,
that fountain of youth, that fountain of fun,
takes leave of the needle, the switchblade, the gun,
the chip on the shoulder, the fork in the tongue,
and there, where the moonlight joins hands with the sun,
where small whirls large, and old follows young,
where the hopes of the world spin, and are spun,
as lamb's bleat from lion's roar, silk out of dung,
where weapons are slighter than light on the water
that glistens and glimmers and jiggles with laughter
and needles less sharp than the pure splash of pleasure
that bursts from the water we all swim together
when anyone falls in the fountain of fun,
the fountain of youth, the fountain of love.

**Self-Defense**
   (1997)


The double-cross of Paul's arms and legs
makes a barricade: it decrees separation
between you and him, it decrees
that his male experience shall be
forever incommensurable with your own.
Why should double-cross mean betray,
when a single cross stands for salvation?

How did Jesus' crucifix wrench his one body
so totally open that, in the absolute
defenselessness of his stance, generations
over millennia longed to become one with him,
yielding up differences, merging individuality
into a communal mystery of salvation?

Why, when you see Paul, must you ponder
all the young men over the centuries
who have ever been fodder for war?
So many returned from it, if not dead,
then missing arms, legs, or soul,
rendered, in defense of their country,
indefensible themselves.
When Paul adopts this position -
the way his elbows jut out,
the way his knees and tibia guard
the vulnerable truth of his body -
why does it unnerve you so?

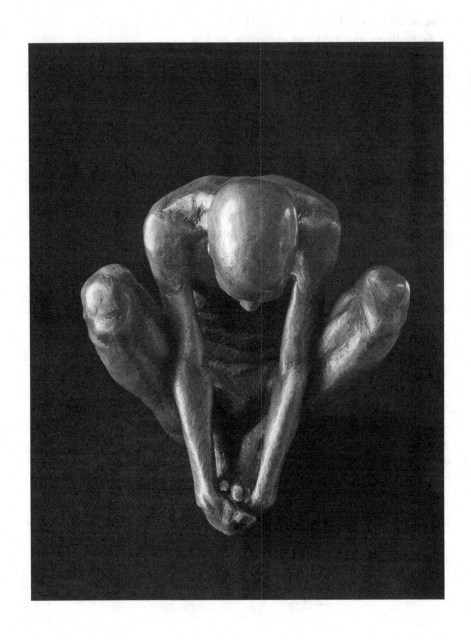

**Ready to Fire**
    (1997)

Like a cocked gun or a taut bow,
this man's heart is ready to go,
ready to blow,
ready to explode him
out of too tight a pose,
into which he has stooped and bent
and bound himself alive,
trying to be what a man must be,
trying to be what a son, husband, father must be,
trying to shove the savage beat of his blood
inside the sweet melody of society,
trying to cram the slam of his fist
inside the kid glove of society.

Every year his responsibilities
weigh heavier, heavier;
every year his muscles
strain harder, harder
to hold back the blast.

Any minute now, his heart will explode.
It is going to blow, it is going to fling
his ballistic soul beyond the horizons of earth,
beyond the entangling atmosphere,
the irresistible gravity.
It is going to hurl him far
into vast and empty expanses of space
where he can finally soar
freed of all orbits and pulls not his own.
Any minute now his heart
will absolve him of love.

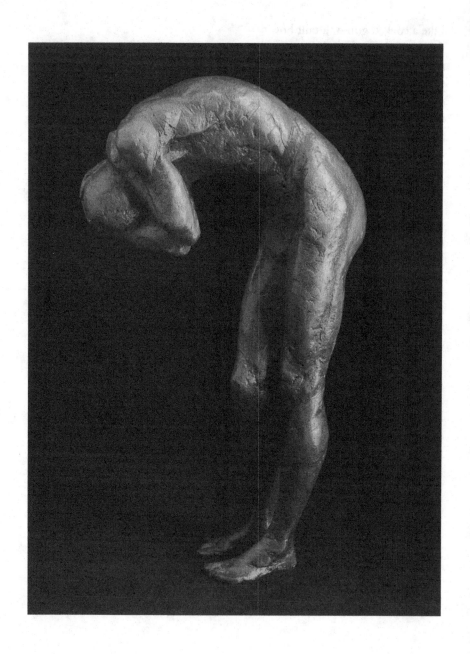

## The Man in the Moon
(1997)

The man in the moon
twists in on himself,
a grape vine whose growth
seems to circle a wandering,
ineluctable center. He cries
for the children of earth.

For a billion years he has
passed over our sleep
with his shifting dance,
whispering secrets to the wild
horses of the sea and the blood.

He has taught us to sing and to dance,
he has taught us to dream,
but the man in the moon
is no match for the rising
sun, the fire in the mind,
the blaze in the hand.

By the clear light of day
he is nothing but a crescent of cloud.
He is nothing and no one, no match
for the bombs and the bullets and tanks,
this man whose moon body bends
and revolves round the human heart,
holding us, loved, in his grief.

## The Girl Who Holds The World in Her Hands
### (1997)

What this little girl holds in her hands
is the whole world to her, and
to this little world she holds,
she's its mother, or God–the source
of all love. She already knows
how much this world needs her,
how only the concentration of her heart
and the continual outpouring of warmth
through her fingers can keep it alive.
Her play is intense and in earnest, she knows
that earth and the adults upon it are fragile,
reliant on her, this is not make-believe:
the whole world is a ball that she holds
in her hands, and all she depends on,
depends for affection on her.

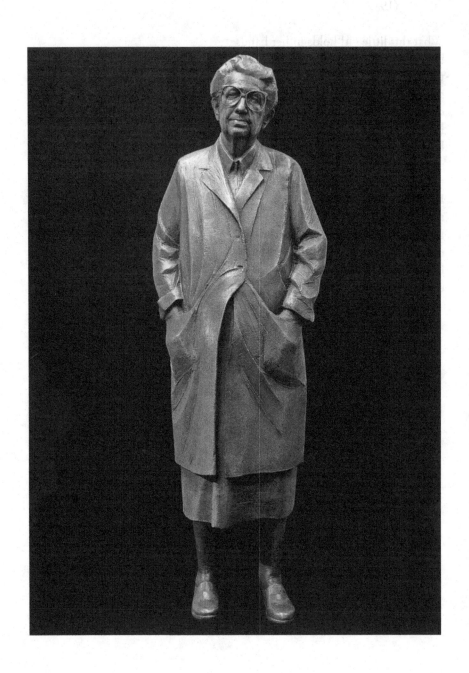

## Dr. June Klinghoffer,
## Soul of Women's Medical College
### (1998)

They struggled,
the women and men
who worked hard to sustain
Woman's Medical College.
In their lineage
Dr. June Klinghoffer
stands steady among us
solid and balanced
on her own two feet,
the soul of that college,
keeper of the legacy,
keeper of the dreams and spirit
of generations who worked
to bring women physicians
into the world. She stands now,
head slightly cocked, hands
thrust into the square pockets
of her white medical robe,
hands that are ready at any moment
to rise up and to teach,
hands ready with practiced knowing
to touch, palpate, treat,
hands ready to pause and to soothe
where they cannot cure.
She stands ready to meet whoever
comes to her, ready to greet
and examine with the cool
skepticism of science, with the warm
welcome of love. Look into her eyes
if you want to receive
the spirit and dream
that she passes on.
Not money but muscle
of mind and of heart
make her pockets deep.

## The Wall of Remembrance
(1993)

What can I build that is big enough
to remember you by?
Mountains and distances vast
as the great gap between us
that could have been filled with such life
when my eyes touched your eyes,
when my hand touched your hand,
when my laugh touched your laugh,
possibilities lost to us now
in the hollow of no sound, the silence
of one hand no longer clapping,
the vast expanse of an absence
I never can span, and yet I must
build from my one little life something big,
something big enough to remember you with.
So I add my one stone to this place,
so small in this landscape of loss,
so small, so beckoning,
it is sure to be joined,
until stone touching stone touching stone,
stones brought by much touching almost to life,
an assembly of stone that may seem to contain
in the depths of each tiniest quivering quark,
the throb and the beat at the heart of all loss.
It will be big enough.

# The Woman Who....

These poems were originally published in chapbook form in 1992. Composed early in the first decade of my marriage with Chris Downing, they capture the vibrancy and playfulness of that phase of our love.

I gratefully acknowledge Chris for all the life and love she has brought to my poetry, as well as to me personally and to my family.

**The Woman Who Swallowed the Moon**
   (1990)

No one had ever warned her, she said,
no one had ever taught her the tune
that one must take care when swilling the moonlight,
one must take care not to swallow the moon.

She said it was simple as a communion wafer
slightly stale and papery thin, that it sat dry and flat
upon the moist and supple surface of her tongue,
the trembling of which she attempted to stop (but could not)
whispering, corpus dei, body of god.

She said it seemed innocent as an after-dinner mint
cool and white and smooth,
a slender disk of marble or of bone,
until saliva licked its curving edge,
and menthol mist arose, dissolving all
her inner surfaces to spaciousness,
painting her, with strokes as tender as a sable brush,
beautiful as the ends of the earth
sky blue, leaf green, incurably remote.

She hoped maybe a moon tree would sprout
and grow and branch out
through her ears or her mouth
heavily laden with fruit.
Or maybe her belly would swell and stretch
in response to a baby's waxing flesh
so that she could give the moon birth.

No one had ever warned her, she said,
no one had ever taught her the tune
that one must take care when swilling the moonlight,
one must take care not to swallow the moon.

## The Woman Who Carries the Atom Bomb in Her Purse
(1990)

Big as a bowling ball, heavy,
a strain on her shoulders, and yet
she carries it gently, as if
attending not to a bomb but a baby.

When she settles the purse down,
whatever surface it rests upon
seems to her as fragrant and fresh
as the head of a newborn child, its skull
still soft from birth, unfinished,
open to injury.

As for the purse,
she keeps it immaculate,
never leaves it alone for a moment.
Like an intensive care unit nurse,
she keeps her eyes glued
to the heart monitor,
vigilantly guarding
her patient's precarious life.

If only it had been a tarantula -
like the big hairy spider
the size of her fist
that scuttled fearfully
under her bed.
She snared it, but simply
to shift it safely to freedom,
a wildness large enough to fully
embrace it.
But no wildness exists in which
one can safely
turn loose this bomb.

Truthfully, it's a burden -
nor can she forget, as others seem to,
the inevitability of the coming explosion.
Sooner or later she's bound to jostle it.

As a child, her dreams were full
of whirring snakes, venomous beings
that flew through the kitchen,
visible only to her.
She would have done anything then
to unveil the danger, to face together
the air raid of vipers, knowing
that only a family united
could hope to prevail.

Even a stampede of tarantulas
could have been shared:
people of every nation, all
dancing their own tarantella,
billions of gyrating bodies
flinging the poison free,
billions of beating feet
stamping the danger to dust.
But there is no dance on earth
wild enough
to defuse the fury of this bomb.

Now she's glad,
in her way,
for the others:
those who are able to not know,
those who are able go on
living their innocent lives.
No one else
besides her
seems to notice
quite
how precious
everything is,
but she can bear
that lone sorrow.
It won't be
very long.

## The Woman Who Walked on Water
### (1991)

It wasn't the water really
She never really wanted
to walk on water.
It was that she wanted somehow
to touch the horizon:
that outstretched edge of the ocean
edge of her limited human vision, edge
of her passing day.

She dreamed of walking
barefoot through the vanishing rose,
through the apricot glow, of the absent sun,
of giving herself to the colors, one
with the edge of all she had ever loved.

She hardly noticed her feet
touching the sea's supple surface,
or that it supported her weight,
so that for the flutter of an eyelid,
the pause before a heartbeat,
she failed to sink.

**The Woman Who Reached Down for a Star**
   (1992)

The star just kept falling, white light
streaking the night sky in almost
instantaneous flight, while the woman's
slow eye trailed behind this sudden
descent to the earth, to the city street,
to her feet: a small rock,
trembling and pulsing and bright.
In her hand, it was not quite
as hot as white fire, not quite
as cold as dry ice, but it bled
incandescence profusely,
as if it would not last the night.

All her life she had wished
to experience this: a star in her hand.
But it shone with a tender fragility,
a tiny, wild thing, newborn, freshly torn
from its dying mother. When she
pressed the small star to her breast,
light flooded her chest.

But in the dark shadow on the other side
of the street, she glimpsed a slight
movement; she knew who
lurked there: her ancient enemy.
At times the CIA sent him, or
the Mafia, at times he came
as a Nazi, or a rapist, or a torturer.
Always he delighted in cruelty:
whether through mild mockery,
fault-finding, seeding small doubts,
spying on her most precious moments,
or engaging in murderous pursuit,
his mission was always to terrorize her,
to extinguish her deeper nature.

But this time she faced him, this time
she did not take flight. She turned as if to

embrace him, but this time she fought.
Furious, she shoved her fist, bright with
the dying light from her orphan star,
into the bleak abyss of his mouth,
that hole into which so much of her
hope has been swallowed and sunk.
What astonishment to see him change,
as the beast and the frog are changed
by the fairy tale kiss, her luminous fist
transforming him, starlight consuming
his face, igniting his brain, the star
itself taking up residence in his empty skull,
from whence it could radiate vigor and lust,
as if all along his flesh has been just
what was needed for a star to feed upon.

## The Woman Who Tamed a Dragon
### (1992)

It wasn't a likely house pet; even half-grown
it was bigger than her whole block. And it's famed
breath of fire could ignite and burn down
every place, person, thing that she loved.
She certainly would not have strolled down
some sunny day to her local SPCA just hoping
to find a young dragon she could adopt.

But this one arrived, breathing out grayness
thicker than smog, the same smoldering gray
that she later would instantly know
as the breath of lost dragons: alone, left to
roam, without family or friend, without home.

She herself had known loss:
these gray clouds were not yet, she knew,
signs of the full conflagration of rage,
though the next little hindrance might well
enkindle those hazardous flames.

But when she tried to hush the fearsome
trembling of her hand, outstretched
for the huge unhappy creature to sniff,
the dragon approached so mournfully,
so cautiously and so clumsily - an enormous
caterpillar, with wings like sails that flapped
in the wind as it walked, lurching from side
to side, slowly - that her heart adopted it:
she gave it a home.

## The Woman Who Led Her Horse Through a Party
### (1991)

There are those who might think she was rude,
but at least she dismounted, and walked.
It wasn't, of course, a visible horse,
yet the party grew hushed
as the large graceful animal strode
with uncivilized ease through their midst.
They could feel the presence
they could not see: it made them think
of how strangely uneasy they were
with their party clothes and their party chatter,
and some, not quite knowing how or why,
reached out to touch the long mane,
the soft nose, the smooth flank
of that horse of transforming power.
Those who reached out were never the same.

The host was dismayed, thought it rude; after all,
the party was stopped. Yet, what if the woman
had simply come riding through, without
bothering to dismount? Riding almost as high
as the sky, the very wind intertwined
with the mane that she held, her thighs
in pounding harmony with the source
of that horse's power, what if she'd simply
come galloping through? In that lightning
flash, how many lives would have been burned,
leaving nothing but seared and scorched earth?
Did the host really think she could choose
to come by herself? What, by hitching
the reins of that horse to some nearby post?
Such a horse has no reins: it can leave,
but it cannot be left.

## The Woman Who Drove Her Car Through The Clouds
(1990)

It was much more confusing than fog
what with the lack of a road,
the missing white lines and reflectors,
the absent companionable tail lights
of cars comfortingly leading the way.
It was zero visibility, and
with nothing to see.
Nor could she steer to any effect
in the accustomed directions,
not to mention the added dimension,
the puzzling question of altitude,
with no built-in controls to correct it.

Yet in spite of the clear lack of traction
she found great satisfaction
in holding tight to the wheel,
which became not a means
but an end in itself:
that comforting circle
reassuringly round like the sun
or the moon or a breast,
like a grapefruit or a peach,
with the radiantly radial symmetry
of a starfish, an octopus, an anemone,
of a spider web, or a flower.
Like the curving long line of the beach
or the orbits of stars,
like a clock or a baseball,
a coin or a marble,
a cup, a saucer, a gong.

And when in fact, somehow,
she drove her car out of the clouds
she went on claiming for years
that it was only because of
the music of the spheres
that she found her way home.

**The Woman Who Set Herself on Fire**
  (1992)

As she tried to explain to the fire,
it had all been a misunderstanding.
It began with an icy cold chill,
then the frustrating way
that even the sun at midday,
the heater, the comforter,
the best woolen sweater,
the new long silk underwear -
everything -
failed to thaw her.

She paced the house to the raucous
beat of her chattering teeth,
while her gloved, mittened hands
(the fingers of which had turned
brilliantly blue)
rhythmically thwacked
her padded arms, thick with layers
of useless insulation.

Hot flashes she had heard of -
she was somewhat prepared to be
spirited off to those tropical climes
for brief and erratic adventures: at least
she would be among her own kind.
But this solo, continuous cold flash
got under her skin.

She struck a match, simply to watch
the flame dance, and to yearn,
since it never occurred to her once
that she might be combustible still,
even in subzero trance.
She thought, without doubt,
that the match that she held
would burn out, as soon
as it touched her cold hand.

She was amazed to see the hand blaze
and then, when the fire leapt up
and twirled around her whole arm,
she just gazed at the eerie intensity,
the transparency of the colors,
elusive and free, as if fire were spirit
that never agreed to live in a body.
She found she could pass her other hand
through the weird radiance,
that nothing was palpably present
(though the other hand too
soon burst into flame) -
she was hypnotized by the mystery,
that something so insubstantial
could cause such searing pain,
and besides,
it had all been a
misunderstanding,
as she tried to
explain
to the fire,
which burned just the same.

## The Woman Who Walked Without Leaving Footprints
### (1990)

Only her footsteps disturbed the first pure
winter snow as it wrapped the whole hill in
powdery silence, as the soft breath of wind
lifted and sifted delicate handfuls, white flakes
wandering gently back down to the earth,
adrift and afloat in the slow language of stars,
while her own breath, snowlike, palpable
and lonely as a cloud, yearned to unite, to curl
up and to fill, kitten soft, each hard empty
shape crushed into the snow by her shoe,
as if to leave the world whole again, and new.

## The Woman Who Lost Her Self
### (1992)

It was something she'd feared from the start.
Someday there'd be nobody home.
She would knock at the door
but no one would answer.
She would call on the phone,
and not even the answering machine
would give her a taped message.
She would find the spare key, or break in,
she would search under beds, inside closets,
but she would find never a trace
of anyone who had ever been home.
She would call the police, wanting
to file a missing person report,
but they would require proof that
such a person at some time actually had
existed. In vain she would search
for some evidence: a birth certificate, diploma,
social security number, signs of wear on
the sheets or the shoes, food that was
opened and partially used. She would
look up old friends and family, but
they'd just shake their heads rather sadly,
wanting to help but unable to recollect
the person she would describe. Until at the end
of her fruitless search, she would sit down,
be still, and steep tea, sipping the memory
of a self she must just have imagined.

**The Woman Who Fell into a Tar Pit**
   (1992)

It wasn't simply a matter of being
in the wrong place at the wrong time,
nor could she blame it entirely on gravity,
since the fact of the matter was
she'd been informed of the law, knew
precisely how excessively heavy her burden
was, that it would predispose her to fall,
that even without the tar, which could be
exceptionally sticky, she wasn't likely to
bounce back at all. She also knew that
convulsions of laughter and the arm, eye,
or ear of a friend could substantially
lighten her burden: in a sense she had chosen
to go on just as she was, letting her back
and shoulders bunch and gather to granite,
the fluid leap and stretch of her feline lips
congeal into a grim immovable brick,
her wrinkled brow lean so far down that,
if it hadn't hardened to lead, it would
have sunk to the ground, as her thoughts
actually did, boulders that slid and crashed
down until, when the avalanche was over,
it would have taken a forklift to rouse them.

Although the tar was thick and viscous
as old glue, it was not a surprise that she sank.
The surprise was how slowly she sank,
how she felt almost buoyant, supported
by all that black goo, so that on the way down
she grew truly delighted to meet the whole crew:
ice age man, saber-tooth tiger, mammoth, tyrannosaurus,
they in their turn were completely enchanted by her
if for no other reason that no one had ever before
enjoyed falling into their pit. Welcoming her, they
picked up their authentic prehistoric instruments
and started to jam and prance, and the tar pit
boiled and bubbled, swayed and danced, and some say
her thoughts grew so airily light that they swirled

up into the night, clear up to the Milky Way
where the stars, when they heard of the rollicking
play, dived down into the fun, and temporarily
abandoned the sky, which turned blacker than tar,
while she and the pit, lit up like a paper lantern
brimful of fireflies, shimmied the night away.

**The Woman Who Threw An Egg at The Cops**
   (1992)

It wasn't a little egg, mind you, or recently laid.
It began centuries back when the boats had brought
kidnapped Africans over the sea - making labor
an affordable commodity for the American home
and plantation. Laid in the middle of the American dream -
the *give me your teeming masses,*
the *crown thy good with brotherhood,*
the *sweet land of liberty,* the *land of the free
and home of the brave* dream - it was a huge
egg of shame, and it grew, each time
a treaty was broken, each time tribes
were slaughtered, each time native people
were evicted from land white Americans wanted.
The egg grew as injustices grew, as hate grew,
it grew in the northern cities, it grew in the south,
with segregation it grew, with the slow dying
of public education, with the market for drugs,
the egg grew. It grew so gigantic that no one
could miss it, yet multitudes somehow went on
pretending they could. "I don't see an egg,
do you?" they would ask, though it totally
obscured their view of the future.

The woman couldn't begin to lift it alone.
It took a legion of women and a lot of sensitive
men, it took a whole generation of children,
it took music and poems and paintings and plays,
it took muscle, heart and a shitload of brains,
but they did what they needed to do. They raised
that egg of our national shame and they heaved it -
threw it straight into the video tape, into the midst
of too many cops beating up one lone man, already
down, his dark skin uniting him with history, with
every African brought by force to America,
the cops' white skins uniting them with history,
with every white master taking by force what
he wanted, and thinking it rightfully his.
The huge egg broke as it hit those tiny

343

cops' unhelmeted heads, but to everyone's shock
it didn't deluge them with sticky albumen, did not
inundate them with sun-yellow yolk. Instead,
an enormous eagle stepped forth, newly hatched,
wings wider already than generations of shame,
beak and talons powerful enough to break
with a single snap, lifetime habits of hatred.
Like the mythical creature it was, the young eagle
flew up as soon as it stepped free of its shell, its wings
slowly stroking the air, making waves of wind as it rose
and the cops who had never seen anything like it before,
gasped and gazed, it was everything all at once
they had ever loved, it was every patriotic song
they had sung, it was fishing and hunting and hiking,
it was their daughter's first laugh, their son's hands
first clapping, it was the super bowl and the world series,
their mother's soft breast, their father's strong hand,
their first romance, and in a kind of trance,
they helped the fallen man stand, as, arm-in-arm,
they watched the long-awaited ascent of that great American bird.

## The Woman Who Cultivated Snails
### (1992)

It was the basil that did it.
Many plants, over the years,
had been mercilessly
munched to the ground by armies
of snails, yet the gardener
eschewed the small poison pellets
that could have repelled them, not
because of concern for the earth,
or kinship with life, both rather
abstract in the face of the
violent death by snail swarm
of a plant that she'd placed in the
ground with her own two hands,
that she'd fertilized, watered,
pruned, and watched over with love,
but because of her eight year old
dog, whose gold leaping laugh
was more beautiful than a thousand
flowers, and who would most
certainly eat poison pellets,
as he ate landscape rock, as he
dug up each fresh planted bulb
just to be sure by means of
his own reliable proboscis
that nobody got sneaky and
buried a bone in its stead.
It is also true that she never
intentionally murdered a snail;
at worst, she tossed one or two
of them over the hedge and
into the canyon, knowing full well
that once they had tasted her
garden, they would henceforth
regard the tough canyon weeds
with a full-bodied sneer, and
come slithering back to
enjoy her more civilized fare.

It was the basil that did it, two
bold sprigs of basil in a garden
where herbs had always been doomed,
two bold new heroes spreading
their leaves to the sun, wriggling
their young roots down into new
ground, verdantly alive, willing
and able to grow,
but mowed down by morning,
when a mob of rapacious
snails was just passing through.

After the young basil died, the
next snail she spied was seized and
transported to "yard recycling,"
with deportation and permanent
relocation weighing heavily
on her mind, but the snail had
no more sense than to delight
in the ride, extending its
exquisitely sensitive
antennae and stretching and
leaning out from its shell, as
a human passenger might
lean out from the wicker basket
under a hot air balloon,
watching with charmed fascination
the ground above which it flew.

 "Snail," she said "your people
are no longer welcome in
my garden," then watched with
surprise as that supple and
vulnerable body shrank back
into its shell, as those valiant
antennae recoiled, and in that
moment she knew that nowhere
in the world was there any garden
that grew a yield more precious
than her own trusting and curious snails.

## The Woman Who Rides the Hills
### (1991)

This grass all along the hills south of Sacramento
fair-haired, translucent, bleached and blurred by the
unblinking sun, this is the gold of which the rush never told.
It spills from these hills, clings to their voluptuous
shoulders and thighs, clothes their smooth flanks with
animal softness, like the fleece of a mythical beast.

Who could resist it, or want to? Not the woman
who willingly rubs her cheeks along the furred
folds of these hills, strokes them with open palm,
slides alongside and against them, touches her own
breast, belly, rib to their tawny loins. Not the
woman who sits astride, who rolls and rocks
with the hills, rides and is tossed, climbs astride
again and again, and rides, rides, rides until
she and the hills together, roaring the gold
of their pleasure, swallow the setting sun.

## The Woman Who Ran Out of Tears
(1991)

It wasn't as if she hadn't known loss:
she knew absence better than her own tongue
and teeth, everything she reached for eventually
vanished, but somehow she thought tears would be
different. Tears were Old Faithful to her, the one
absolutely reliable fountain: the river that would
never run dry, the reservoir never depleted.

As a child, she did this terrific imitation
of the Pacific Northwest: you should have seen her,
drizzling for days, weeks, months; kids from all over
the neighborhood came, it was like having their own
local rainforest, right there in the midst of the city.
They could touch moss and fern, smell pine sap,
hear old wood decomposing. As soon as they
sensed the comforting drip of her tears, they snuggled
their roots deep into her world of green,
and relaxed. They could breathe.

It was a shock the day the tears stopped.
It wasn't as if she hadn't heard of the drought:
that year even the grasshoppers joked that the great
Lake Shasta wasn't knee-high to their kind,
smaller reservoirs cupped nothing but dust,
while the hills, gardens, lawns dried to dull brown
(except where a spray of paint tried
to impersonate the lost living green),
and whole species of trees simply died out.

The absence of tears was a lasting drought in her life,
long after the rain came back and the lakes refilled,
yet she seemed to grow even closer to the missing
tears than to the actual ones that had coursed
down her cheek. Mesmerized by moving water,
she would sit beside ocean, stream, sprinkler,
or fountain, and dream: about tears, about water,
how it transforms to fit the container it's in,
how it catches and tosses back pleasure

from its bright diamond facets, how it washes
away whatever is no longer needed, yielding fully
to the thirst of the moment, how its joy in
movement is transparent, whether as current,
wave, ripple, splash, foam, wherever it goes,
without needing to stay, it's completely at home.

## The Woman Who Planted Daffodils
   (1997)

It started small, you have to understand,
it was only a few bulbs the first year,
maybe a dozen or so, but the vision of those
yellow trumpets bursting out of the ground
had the power to banish the cold winds,
the ice and the snow. It was as if
she was incubating the spring,
as if the seasons were under her care,
as if by breaking the ground with her hands
she could bring back the sun.

The next year she planted a hundred or two,
and the next year a thousand; before very long
she was busy all winter burying bulbs,
and praying for peace in the world,
praying that there be no more torture,
no more painfully foreshortened lives
for good friends with cancer,
no more homelessness for the poor.

She patted down the cold earth
over yet another incipient daffodil,
knowing every bulb really was
an occasion of light, was
what she'd learned as a girl a sacrament
could be: a sign that accomplishes
the transformation it signifies.
If an ordinary woman like herself
could single-handedly contrive
the uprising of a million daffodils,
there was no limit to the revolutions
others might ignite.

## The Woman Who Laughed at Death
(1997)

Not that complete annihilation was her idea of a joke,
nor that death's usual preludes brought a grin to her face -
she was not amused by death usurping
powers toddlers found hard-won:
command of the toilet, the cup and the spoon,
control over clothing and shoes,
escape from the crib,
the freedom to choose.

What did make her laugh was death's habit
in the midst of the actual joy of her life,
of trying to grab her undivided attention,
death all dressed up like a Halloween child
waving sheets and skulls. It made her aware
how kindred in spirit she and death really were:
both of them longing for so much more life
than life would allow.

# Writing In Air With No Ink:
## Selected Haiku
## (2004-2007)

The following haiku are all separate poems, even though I have chosen to place more than one on a page.

For several years most of my poetry practice took the form of haiku. I am immensely grateful for the tradition and discipline of the haiku, which helps me to enter the present moment and connect with my senses and the natural world.

Haiku came to me as a gift from children. I had been volunteering in the local elementary school, helping first and second graders write poems. A mother of one of the students introduced me to a childrens' book titled *Basho and the Fox*. I loved the story so much that I started reading more haiku. When I came across William Higginson's *Haiku Handbook* I was a goner. I am so grateful to the long lineage of haiku poets and to the natural world for the joy this practice has brought to my life. I also have focused on haiku in my work with children since then, and what a beautiful experience that has been.

wind whipped lake
one yellow maple leaf
riding the waves


playground near ocean --
all day the swings and the waves
rising and falling.


morning sun slipping
between trees...ah!  Spring grass
Just starting to rise


New Year's Day ashes
last year's broken branches
still smoldering


late afternoon:
day's last gold light gleaming
through winter branches


morning walk
footprints in fresh snow
half moon in sky


snow-covered beach
raven perched on driftwood
gazing out to sea


melting icycles
reflecting last orange light
sun drops behind hills

small girl shaking head
back and forth back and forth
ponytails slap cheeks


between stacks of books
cat batting hair band
all around desk


all along the road
trees and branches lie broken:
storm over


woman on couch
her thumb caressing the page
she's about to turn


march morning
snowflakes float up down around
blossoming plum tree


light spring rain
sprinkling lake
birds murmuring


duck rearing up
white and black wings flapping
skimming across lake


april wind
ruffling lake surface
ducks rocking

tour group wanders
through ruins - butterfly wanders
through tour group


mountain road
car driving up switchbacks
mist drifting up gorge


small white petals
fragrance rising from trail
clouds cover lake


man on bicycle
Hawaiian shirt billowing
in summer breeze


golden poppies
a grazing fawn lifts her face
into sunlight


early summer
big black slug beginning
to cross trail


New year's roadside
ginseng tea bottle broken
scattered shards shining


flashlight on dark road:
sound of wind in winter trees
rising and falling

mountain clearing
wet trail shining
in winter sun


neckbands gleaming
two wild geese glide over
morning meadow


water swirling –
two cormorants circle
the ferry pier


longest day
sun hides
behind clouds


summer lake
trail blossoming
stray socks


summer sunset
the cat closes her eyes
and purrs


driving past
"congested area" sign
her nose fills up


silence:
September wind swings
the big bell

doe pausing
in morning mist
ears open wide


the same rain --
sad tears, happy tears drip down
the two pumpkin faces


airplane lit pink by dawn
passing waning half moon
new year beginning


predawn dark
you and I and the cat
breathing together


between her house
and my house
footprints in the snow


doe pausing in snow
her dark eyes
following us


sipping jasmine tea --
fragrance of night flowers
floating through morning


geese on frozen lake
some standing
some lying down

muddy trail
deep footprints
filling with rain


through ferry porthole
two suns rising -- one in air
one on water


February chill
early cherry blossoms
shivering


motorcycle
curving around the lake
sound fading


driving to vet's
dog barking cat howling
eagle swoops over


bumper sticker
"Kerry 2004"
vanishing in mist


cormorant in mist
head turning this way
that way


morning ferry
wake vanishing
in the mist

ferry car deck:
by the "spill response" barrel
a puppy peeing


excavator jaws still --
workmen standing nearby
chewing candy bars


climbing the mountain—
beyond the crest
more mountains


you and I stepping
from woods into clearing --
sun from behind clouds


just for this moment
a tiny gap in the clouds:
mountain creek sparkling


slug on the trail
antennae stretching out
shrinking back


a bare white table
two empty white chairs
beyond them the sea


scooping dog poop:
pear blossom petals
drift by

waning half moon
deer leaping through daisies
snow on distant mountain


broken foxglove
resting petals on wet log:
falling water sound


"keep out" sign
wild daisies growing
through the log fence


wind tossing
blackberry blossoms --
bees hanging on


after graduation
leaves rustling overhead
beyond them, blue sky


the road ahead
tall grasses on both sides
waving in the wind


crescent beach morning:
heron standing still
in still water


sunlit pickup truck
spaniel sleeping on man's chest
wind ruffling their hair

fir branch over lake
small bird perched upside down
swings in autumn sun


two dogs drink
from one bowl
tails wagging in unison


roar of car passing --
overhead the cedar frond
barely stirs


before crossing --
a squirrel pausing at road's edge
one foot in the air


biting off wet grass
the ewe lifts up her head
to chew and to gaze


lone swan's call
floating on gray lake
gray sky


black morning sky–
white dog gazing down stairs
tilting her head


misty morning
white wings over swamp
flapping then settling

big old Maple tree
limbs covered with ravens --
winter foliage


snow geese in field
some standing, some settling down –
snow on mountain


argument on the trail
rain turning to hail


hush – by the lake
heron standing so still
you barely see it


after tears, sun—
through kitchen window
winter branches shine


whoosh! heron rising
blue feathers spread-- clouds
dispersing from sky


pier floating in mist
wild  ginger buds  almost
ready to open


robin hopping
across roadside ditch
March morning

all down Prune Alley
the plum trees teaching my heart
how to blossom


a trapped bat swooping
out the door into the dark –
April moon-set


ripples of sunlight
caressing
the bottom of the lake


two fluffy white dogs
their black noses
just touching


millipede
meandering across trail –
sky clearing


spring rain
white dogs stopping
to smell the flowers


deep tree shadows–
a bird darting out
into the daylight


summer morning
light off the lake rippling
up and down tree trunks

a cry of surprise
the boy's fishing rod
rearing up


sun on madronas
peeled back bark-skin exposing
smooth chartreuse curves


white feathers floating
down mountain creek: full moon
midsummer morning


yellow leaf
lying face down on the trail
fall beginning


last spring's sap
still shining on the fir trunk
autumn morning


autumn rain
wet pears on a pear tree
raven settling


paper cup lying
sideways in rain puddle
half empty, half full


waning harvest moon
the first of the migrating swans
float on the pond

marsh grass reflections
waver and break –
leaf landing on water


above the marsh grass
writing in air with no ink –
the dragonfly's path


sound of the creek –
fern fronds stretch out
to touch one another


fuschia shadows
swing on the bell –
bright morning wind


raven on fencepost
spiderweb silvered by mist


wind dying down
lake waves still slapping
gray rocks


grey clouds
sweeping over the mountain
leaves over the road


the wind and the kids
the kids and the wind
all the way home

pale yellow light
through morning clouds
soft twitter of birds


through the cat door
cat pausing, stepping out
into the rain


through rain-streaked window
bending and thrashing of trees


in the lake
misty reflections
of misty trees


even the birds
soften their voices
this misty morning


weeks of rain, now sun:
boy in a red vest
paddling a red canoe


last night's rain
dripping from fir branches
into ferns


school garden
sunflower bowing
under a crow's weight.

through winter branches
the white dog singing
to the moon


with every breath
more Paris – climbing
Eiffel Tower


winter sun
through the same kitchen window
as last night's moon


Full moon rising
through kitchen window –
sink empty of dishes


honk sound then six
swans gliding in silence
touch their reflections.


the hills reflection
barely rippling


playing peek-a-boo
behind silver clouds
November moon.


kitchen counter
in moonlight – the refrigerator
motor stopping

nibbling pear flesh
off the slender core –
juicy fingertips.


dog racing through waves
between sunset in wet sand
and sunset in sky


small bird
flitting from one bare branch
to another


past the "trail" sign
its arrow pointing
the other way


through the branches
ferry lights and their reflections
nearing the dock


perched on a fencepost
a lone hawk
staring into the mist


behind hay truck
bits of loose hay
spinning and swooping


after lovemaking
she picks up the strewn
tulip petals

page with no poem—
on the snow-covered mountain,
the untracked white road

# Magic Carpet

(2007)

Some say the body of god
is a thin white wafer that melts
on your tongue.

But I say the body of god
is unfathomable
darkness in which

far-flung galaxies
blossom and slowly unfold
their intricate worlds of light

a Turkish rug
into whose filaments of silk
some country girl's infinitely patient fingers
weave the traditional flowers.

Your bare toes touch
the fearful symmetries of her arduous hours
as you walk with your willing heart
the body of god.